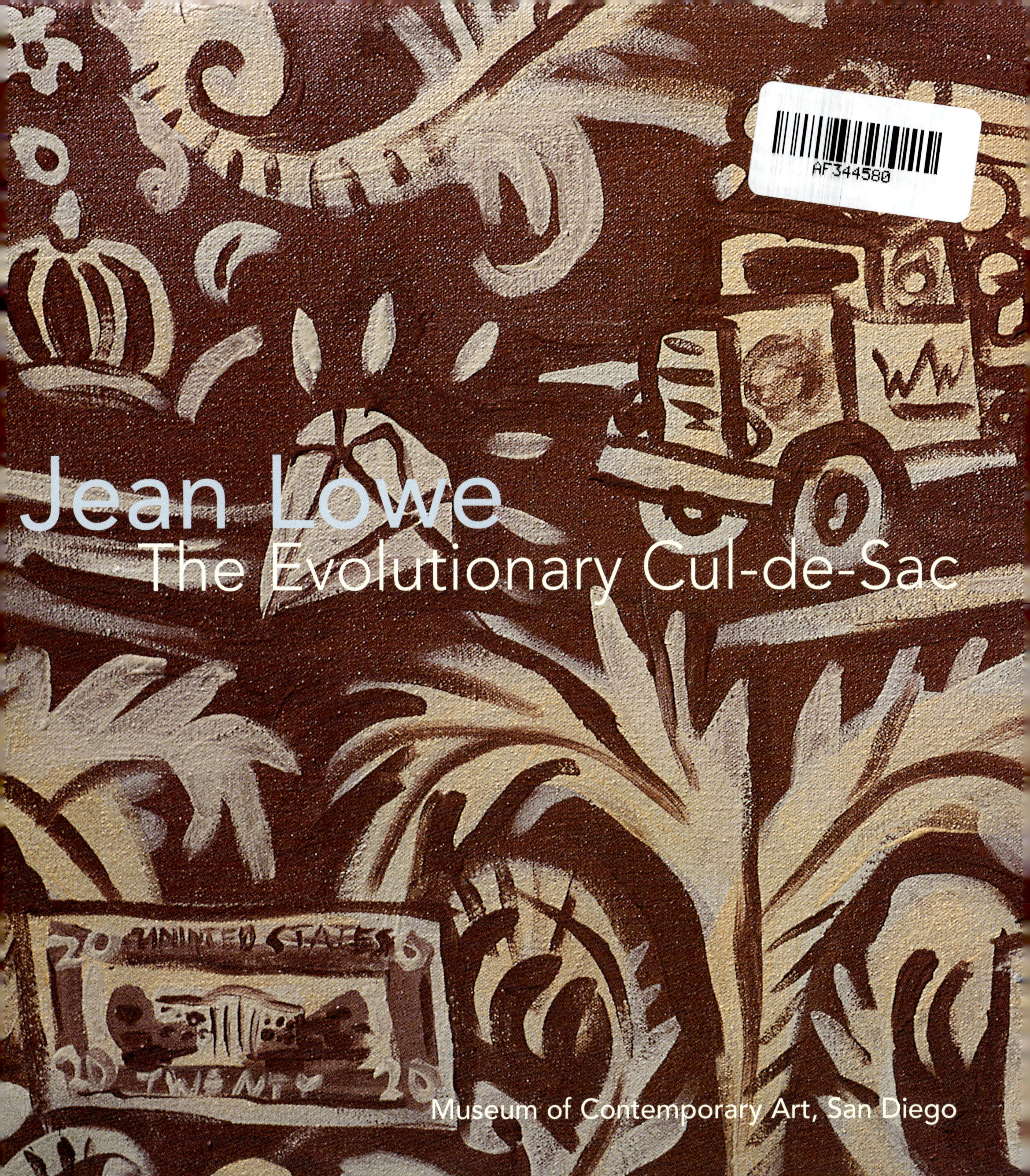

# Jean Lowe
## The Evolutionary Cul-de-Sac

Museum of Contemporary Art, San Diego

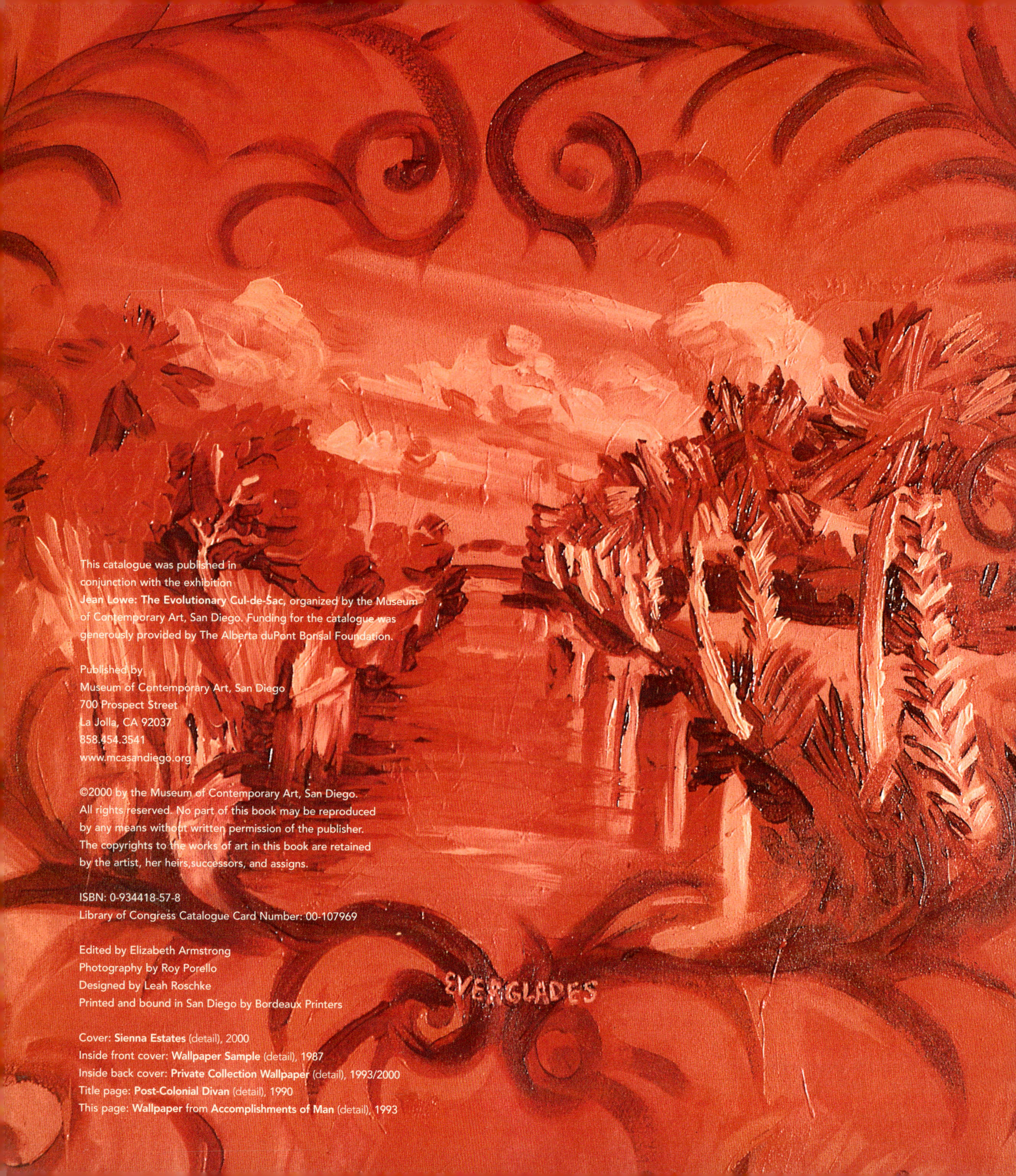


This catalogue was published in
conjunction with the exhibition
**Jean Lowe: The Evolutionary Cul-de-Sac**, organized by the Museum
of Contemporary Art, San Diego. Funding for the catalogue was
generously provided by The Alberta duPont Bonsal Foundation.

Published by
Museum of Contemporary Art, San Diego
700 Prospect Street
La Jolla, CA 92037
858.454.3541
www.mcasandiego.org



ISBN: 0-934418-57-8
Library of Congress Catalogue Card Number: 00-107969

Edited by Elizabeth Armstrong
Photography by Roy Porello
Designed by Leah Roschke
Printed and bound in San Diego by Bordeaux Printers

Cover: **Sienna Estates** (detail), 2000
Inside front cover: **Wallpaper Sample** (detail), 1987
Inside back cover: **Private Collection Wallpaper** (detail), 1993/2000
Title page: **Post-Colonial Divan** (detail), 1990
This page: **Wallpaper** from **Accomplishments of Man** (detail), 1993

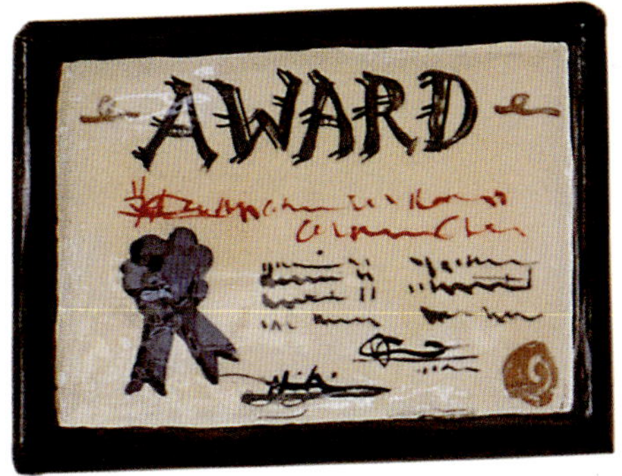


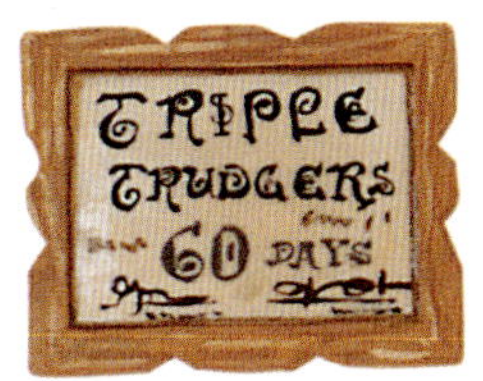


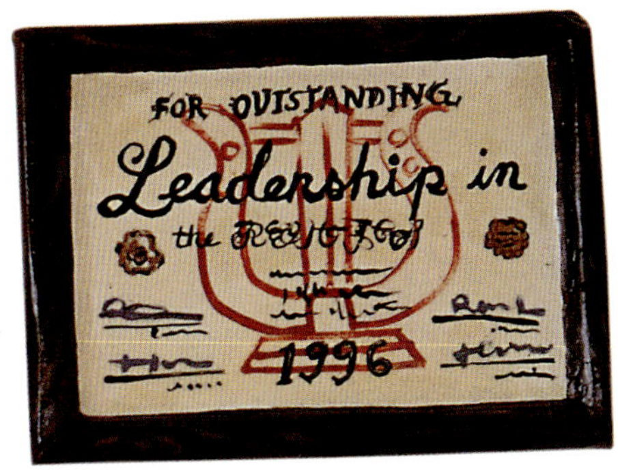


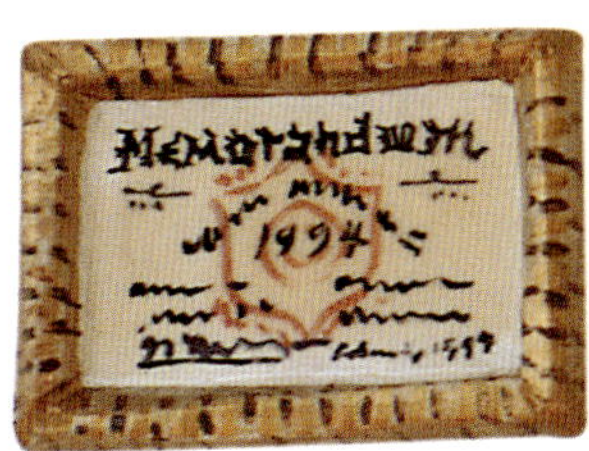


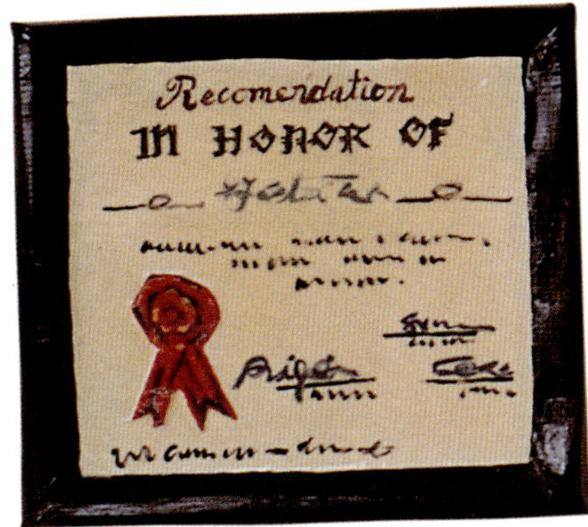


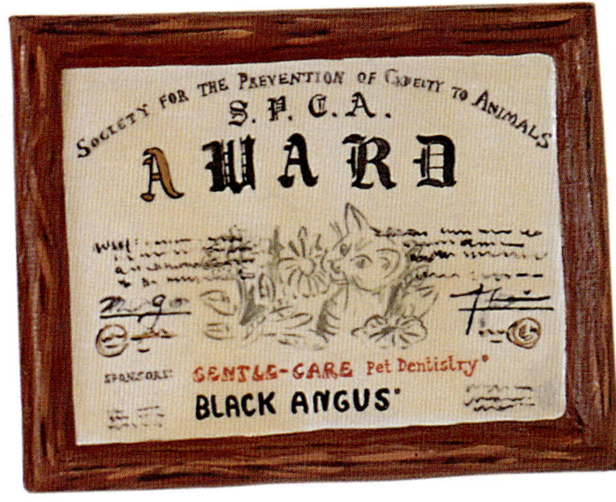


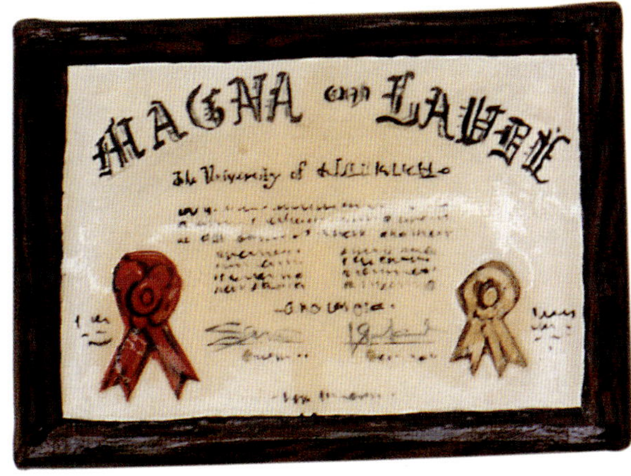


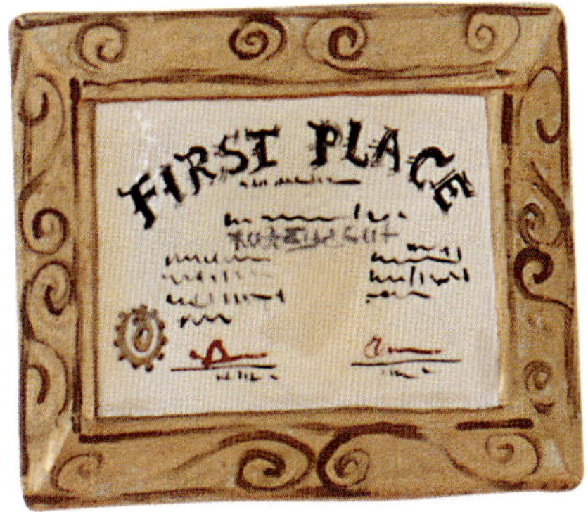


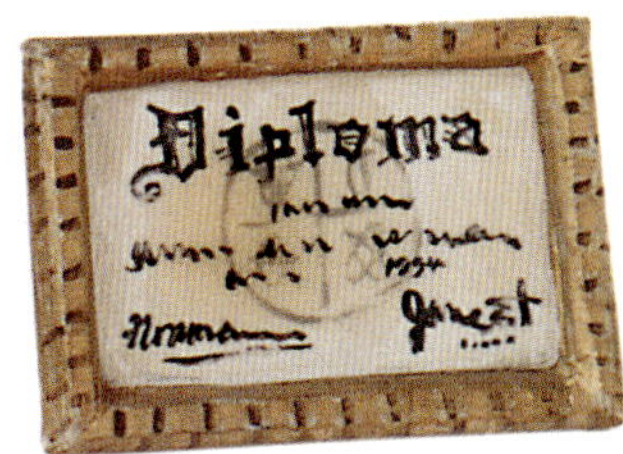


Awards, 1994–1996

# Foreword and Acknowledgments

When we first approached Jean Lowe about showing her work at our downtown Museum, it was with the notion that we would present a selection of highlights from her career. Although willing to subject herself to this kind of survey, Jean's strong desire was also to create a new body of work. The result is this wonderful exhibition, *Jean Lowe: The Evolutionary Cul-de-Sac.* Fusing the old with the new, it provides a humorous and darkly compelling context for exploring the artist's aesthetic and social concerns that, as they have evolved over the years, have inspired and informed her work. The exhibition serves as the blueprint for this publication. Following the layout of the show, it is based on those works that were featured in the galleries at MCA Downtown from June 10 to August 13, 2000.

The figurative cul-de-sac in the exhibition's title refers to a society that is reaching a breaking point in its collective treatment of the land and other species. A significant portion of Lowe's work has been an attempt to illuminate what humans are doing to the natural environment, and to explore the continuum of degradation that is eroding our natural ecosystems. Her landscape paintings—with their dammed-off rivers and encroaching subdevelopments—are subtle reminders of the ever-fragile relationship between humans and the natural world. The Rococo-style, salon-like domestic interiors of Lowe's installations—featuring decorative images of nature on the wallpaper and in their ornamental details—suggest a long tradition idealizing nature and aestheticizing reality. Other works, such as her faux panel paintings and books, use titles and text to challenge—more pointedly—our culture's predatory attitude towards other species and nature.

Two families of MCA Trustees have helped support this project. We are extremely grateful to Trustee Gough Thompson, his daughter Lydia duPont Thompson, and his wife Irene Thompson, as it was their decision to inaugurate the first year of their family's Alberta duPont Bonsal Foundation (with its mission of furthering the careers of outstanding women artists) with a major grant to support this publication, as well as additional support to acquire Lowe's work, *Rancho Dorado,* 2000, for the MCA permanent collection. Also helping make this exhibition and book possible was a generous contribution from MCA Trustee Colette Carson Royston and Dr. Ivor Royston, both of whom have had a long-standing commitment to women artists and to MCA's exhibition programs. In addition, special thanks go to the City of San Diego Commission for Arts and Culture and to the California Arts Council for their support of the interpretive aspects of this exhibition.

We thank Leah Roschke who, working closely with the artist, designed this beautiful catalogue, which is enlivened throughout by Roy Porello's excellent photographs. Mark and Anna Quint of Quint Contemporary Art, the artist's gallery in San Diego, also deserve special thanks for their unstinting support of Jean Lowe, of this project, and of the Museum. We greatly appreciate, as well, those who so graciously lent works to this exhibition: The Bodi Collection, Max and Melissa Elliott, Dietrich Jenny, Quint Contemporary Art, and Holly Solomon Gallery.

The Museum of Contemporary Art, San Diego, is
fortunate to have an outstanding staff and Board of
Trustees, and I extend my thanks to all of them. As
always, we benefit from the counsel and support of
all the members of the board, under the leadership of
President Charles G. Cochrane. On the staff, particular
thanks go to Senior Curator Elizabeth Armstrong and
Curatorial Assistant Allison Berkeley, who are responsi-
ble for the exhibition and this handsome publication.
I would also like to thank Curator Toby Kamps,
Education Curator Kelly McKinley, Community
Outreach Coordinator Gwen Gómez, Registrar
Mary Johnson, Curatorial Coordinator
Doriot Negrette Lair, Lila Wallace Curatorial
Intern Miki Garcia, Preparators Ame Parsley
and Max Bensuaski, Registrarial Assistant Allison
Cummings, and Research Assistant Tamara Bloomberg
for their assistance on this project. I am grateful as well
to Director of Development and Special Projects Anne
Farrell, and the other talented members of the develop-
ment staff, as well as to Deputy Director Charles Castle
and the administrative staff. Their professional contri-
butions, as always, have been invaluable.

Most of all, however, I thank Jean Lowe, for the work
she has created and for her thoughtful devotion to its
presentation. She awakens us to issues of the utmost
social and political importance, but does so with an
uncommon level of talent, grace, energy, subversive
humor, and quiet passion.

*Hugh M. Davies*
*The David C. Copley Director*

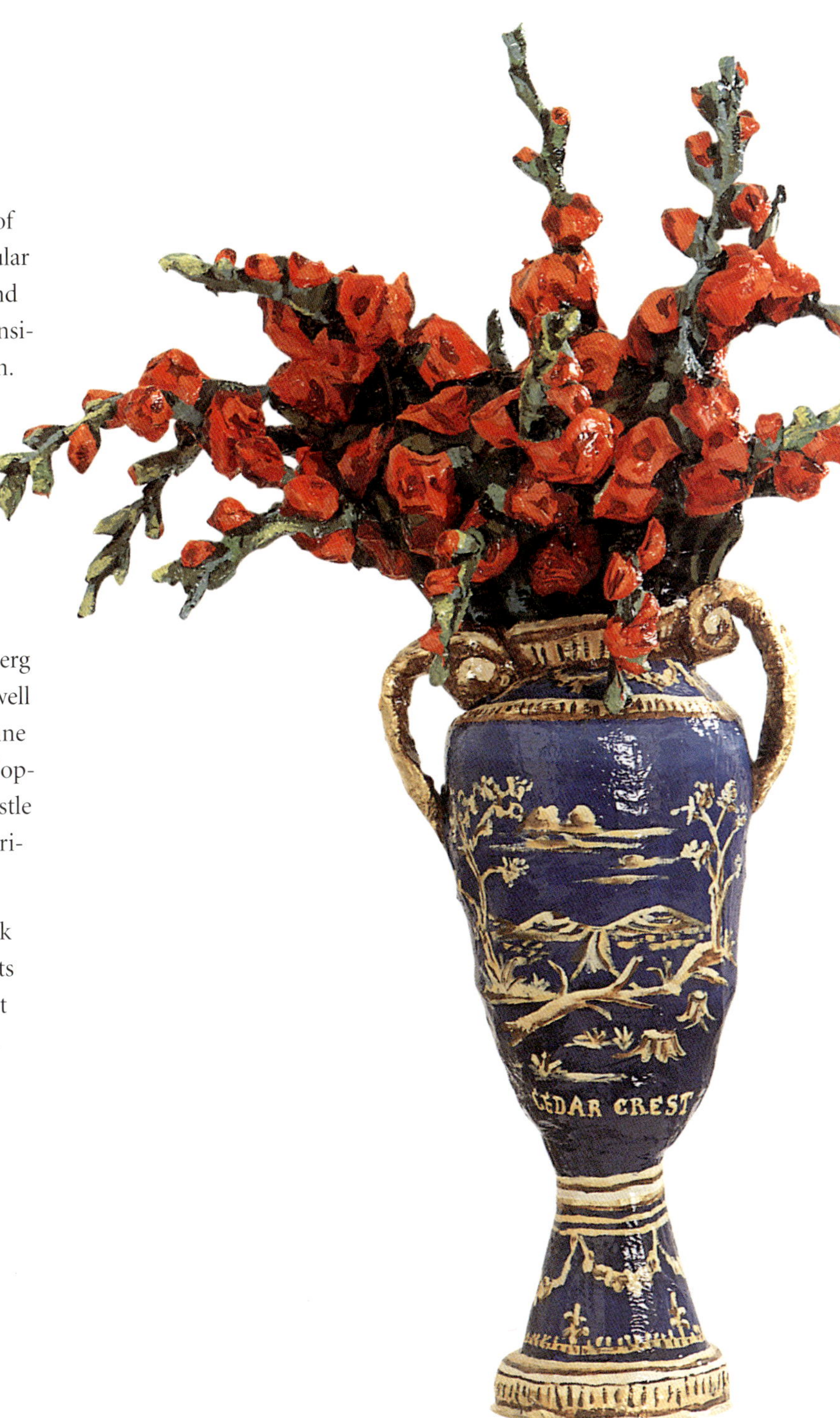

**Bouquet**, 2000

# An Interview with Jean Lowe

by Elizabeth Armstrong

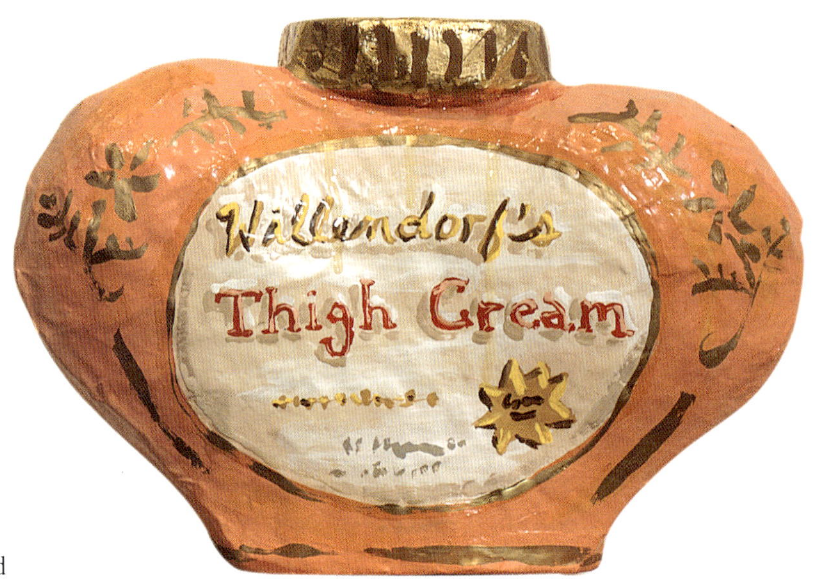

**Personal Care Product**, 1994

**EA:** You know Jean, I have a theory that your father was a real-estate developer and that you grew up in a white modernist house.

**JL:** Almost. My father did his best work with the criminally insane. He was a psychiatrist. But we lived in Palo Alto.

**EA:** In a . . . ?

**JL:** A nice old house.

**EA:** Okay, so much for that theory. Jean, I thought we might just walk through the exhibition, at least to start this conversation. The first thing people see when they enter the show is a wall of trophies, with all kinds of awards, diplomas, and certificates. It's kind of like walking into a doctor's office and seeing all their framed credentials. Why did you put these works on the opening wall?

**JL:** These were originally made for the offices of inSITE94 and were meant to confer status on this ambitious art organization . . . At the same time, they clearly pique the need for that status and stability. These pieces function the same way here.

**EA:** Following up on that, in the next room are four new, monumental paintings. These canvases, which have the scale of eighteenth- and nineteenth-century history paintings, actually feature twentieth-century landscapes. Could you talk a little about these works— in terms of process and content?

**JL:** First of all, my decision to make these big paintings was a desire to do something both serious and fun, and, given the opportunity to do the show at the museum,

to make work that didn't necessarily have to have any commercial appeal—hence, the huge scale—where I was really able to engage with the paint. I wanted to do paintings that were super loose, that when you walked up to them the image might dissolve. While the subject matter is harsh, I was thinking about what would be pleasurable to do and, hopefully, to look at.

**EA:** Pleasurable for you, in terms of making them?

**JL:** Yes, but even though I was very much thinking about the central pleasure of paint, I was also balancing that with critical content. I think of them as generic Southern California landscapes, but they all depict specific scenes in northern San Diego County. In terms of process, I spent some time scouting around finding places that seemed dramatic to me and then I took multitudes of photographs at various times of day.

**EA:** These scenes are similar in that they are all differ- ent kinds of housing developments in the making.

**JL:** Right, they are all virgin landscapes in the process of being transformed to meet our desire for more housing.

**EA:** Why are you interested in painting degraded landscapes?

**JL:** It's the document of a particular time and place. I was thinking of Hudson River School paintings . . . and of trying to create a balancing act between a panoramic, visual beauty, and lush paint, with the irony of the depicted landscape.

**EA:** How does the scale play into this?

**JL:** It imbues the scene with importance, like it or not.

**EA:** So back in the studio, you pieced together the photographs and made collages, then made your choice of which views you were going to paint.

**JL:** And in some cases, combined or collapsed things.

**EA:** Okay, that was one of my questions. In terms of process, do you make sketches first before you begin to paint?

**JL:** These preliminary photographs are my sketches. On the canvas I only very loosely map out a horizon line, or plot out the grossest kind of "directions." And then it's simple underpainting before flying across the canvas. Sky first, then land left to right. I hope it doesn't look this methodical.

**EA:** I would say that, looking at the way the paint just seems to move across those canvases, they absolutely convey the pleasure of painting.

**JL:** Thank you. It's really a focused kind of looking and energy that is difficult to maintain.

**EA:** Also in this gallery, you painted three benches that were made, in part, to encourage viewers to feel free to sit down and take in these huge paintings. You painted them with a sort of cartoony wood grain, which feels very "pop." Did you mean for these to suggest a way of reading the paintings, or to raise questions about the nature of painting today?

**JL:** Well, for one thing, I was actually thinking of the viewer's comfort. But these oversized benches play to the scale of the paintings, and, combined, they playfully reinforce the status of museum, and, of course, the status of painting.

**EA:** It all sort of mimics the way large paintings are presented in historical museums.

**JL:** Yes, but because this is a modern gallery, the benches are Danish modern.

**EA:** There is some humor, of course, in presenting these huge paintings, with their faux gilt frames, in this modern space. It's well known your work gets people talking about its subject matter—about social and environmental themes, etc. We'll return to this, but I'm interested in talking a little about aesthetic issues in your work. There was a term from the late 1980's, which I think has been associated with your work, and I'm curious if you feel it fits, and that is the term "Bad Painting." I'm curious if you identified with that term.

**JL:** No. I think a lot of that really was bad painting. I've always reacted viscerally to the physicality of paint but I'm not necessarily drawn to the personal, poetic subject matter, which I think "Bad Painting" was about. There was, or is, however, the shared interest in using what was considered a gauche medium: paint; and genre: representation. And add to that, in my case, this non-art-world subject matter and you're walking the line in terms of taste . . . and respect.

**EA:** Well, also, I don't know when you started using papier-mâché, but that wouldn't exactly be a medium of choice for artists working at that time.

**JL:** Yes, I agree. It would have been something like text and photo, or meticulously arranged found objects. No sign of the hand.

**EA:** So, when you were in graduate school (at UCSD), was it theoretical and conceptual work that was emphasized the most? And were you consciously working outside of that?

**JL:** Yes, I knew I had this real attraction to painting, and was determined to get it out of the box, get it to engage, be conceptual and carry the specific kind of social subject matter I'm committed to.

**EA:** So you knew by the time you were in graduate school that you wanted to paint, and that you wanted to make work that dealt with social issues of importance to you. Would you say that those issues have changed a lot over the years?

**JL:** I think it's been a pretty organic development. I started off addressing specific animal related issues and gradually have gone towards broadening the conversation and embracing a little more ambiguity. Setting up a conversation rather than an argument. Attitudes toward our treatment of other species certainly cross over to our regard for the environment. And that to be concerned about any of this is considered soft or feminine naturally leads into broader questions about the patriarchal, Judeo-Christian way of encountering the world.

**EA:** Any concerns about using the visual arts as your vehicle to address social themes?

**JL:** Sure, but overall, I think there are many ways to affect change. And one way is to bring the discussion to an art world, cultural level. It's not placards on the street corner, it's addressing a different audience. Not to belabor it, street level activism frequently affects change; but people who look at and collect art also run powerful corporations.

**EA:** Let's move upstairs. There are several works in the galleries that feature salon-like installations. A salon is a room for conversation, and your work certainly poses questions and suggests a dialogue. Your salons tend to be late eighteenth-century in terms of style and decoration. I'm curious about the particular references you are making by focusing on that historical period and on the salon in general.

**JL:** One of the things that has been a concern to me all along is trying to make work that can address a wide audience. I've tried hard to be non-elitist, and, ironically, this kind of Rococo, decorative style, which was originally intended for an aristocratic class, does provide a way to initiate conversation. The notion of using a style that was consumed by an elite class—and hijacking it by switching romanticized images of nature and animals with related but contemporary imagery; and to use that to critique not domination by social class, but by an elite species, has a nice symmetry. I also

like that both are somewhat theatrical, and seductive in their familiarity. Using a 'historical' space where you may actually stand on some of the work is an attempt to engage and disarm the viewer. And in an installation, things sort of visually unfold and I think that lends itself to a conversational reading.

**EA:** It's like entering a period room and being invited to poke around. And you're saying the intent of that is to make the audience comfortable and to enter into what is going on in the room?

**JL:** Yes, and more specifically, enter into the content of the work, which is considered within this decorative framework. Part of this is just about entertainment. I've grown to respect that quality more inherently. But for the pleasure decoration affords, it's also able to carry pointed subject matter. Look at the eighteenth century. Of course it's devalued in contemporary art.

**EA:** You mean that the decorative in art is considered pejorative?

**JL:** Yeah, or simply feminine or gay. But my point is that because it's familiar, it's accessible. You know, even the most abstract minimalist painting becomes decoration once it goes into a collector's home. At base, it challenges an art-world hierarchy and a general elitism of work that is really only legible to a minority of people. I certainly hope to interest that minority in my work, but also attract a wider viewership as well.

**EA:** What kind of reactions would you say audiences have to your work?

**JL:** Oh, you know, there are people who love it and people who hate it. And those who read it as being too didactic and those who read it as being too fluffy.

**EA:** Hence your ambiguity. Well, the decorative aspects of your work are certainly distinctive. And although there still aren't that many artists embracing the decorative, I would say that is changing in recent years.

**JL:** You could cite a whole raft of youngish Los Angeles artists who quote the decorative, for instance Lari Pittman. Or the artists I've shown with at Holly Solomon Gallery in New York.

**EA:** It seems to me that you've given a lot of thought to using parody in your work. Why do you think it is so effective to use humor to deal with serious subject matter?

**JL:** Well, I don't think this is true for all issues. If you're talking about what are now, or have been, condoned art-world issues, like those around AIDS, gender or race, you don't necessarily need humor. But if you're talking about something like factory farming, which no one likes to think about and everybody is implicated in, you don't want to sound like a shrew . . . and you've just automatically got to be prepared for the most defensive audience. If you don't want to preach, you've got to have guile.

**EA:** In the upper galleries, there is a wall of panel paintings and a wall of books. These combine, for the most part, provocative or deadpan images with text. I'm curious where you get your ideas for these works. Are the images or text pulled from research and reading and everyday stuff? I'm also thinking about how the images and text are often disjunctive, which is part of their humor, of course. But where did you come up with titles such as the *ABC's of the Afterlife* or *A Boy's First Duck* or the *Encyclopedia of Elective Surgery?*

**JL:** I start by thinking around a theme. I keep a big picture file, and I might thumb through various books and catalogues. Sometimes it starts with a phrase, sometimes with an image. Taken as a whole, the text and imagery of the books riff out a humorous critique of contemporary mores.

**EA:** I was thinking about the panel painting called *The Evolutionary Cul-de-Sac,* where there's an image of three tough looking British blokes hanging outside of a building, smoking.

**JL:** Actually, there are five guys: two sitting or squatting. They're smoking a joint.

**EA:** Evolutionary Cul-de-Sac, which you've written across the bottom of the painting, is such a wonderful term. Could you have been just as likely to use that term over the image of a woman lying on a beach chair or across an image of suburban sprawl?

**JL:** Sure. These guys are going nowhere, wasting time, and by extension suggest a culture, society, or species up against the wall. But there are endless images that could suggest the same thing.

**EA:** I guess I'm asking if you are making work that suggests answers to some of the questions that you're posing?

**JL:** I haven't ever really done work that poses a positive model—although I think there are answers, I just think that's eminently more difficult. Also, when you have a culture that is involved in so many appalling practices, it seems like attempting to create an awareness of these things is already a pretty full agenda.

**EA:** There's hardly a shortage of subjects to explore.

**JL:** I think the optimism of the work exists in its formal characteristics—the pleasure of the paint; the presence of the hand. I mean, how would you do a positive artwork that suggests a return to, say, a regional economy?

**EA:** Sounds like a book to me Jean.

**JL:** That's the thing about doing books. You can slip something frank and straightforward into a grouping and not be too heavy handed. Also, because they're small and somewhat inconsequential, there's the playfulness of loose associations and the disarming nature of humor.

**EA:** One of the things that you do in your work is to question our basic values and assumptions. By working against the grain aesthetically, of course, you are doing that too.

**JL:** Well, it seems like currently artists can quote Duchamp 'till the cows come home. That's terrific, but to what end? Or artists can address the kinds of topics I'm interested in, in a tough and critical but hands off fashion—think Hans Haacke, Allan Sekula, or Alfredo Jaar. That's great. But I want to frame my aesthetic and argument on my own terms. It's girl power translated to the visual arts. The feminine can coexist with strength and intellect just as juicy paint and a seductive object can carry conceptual and serious subject matter.

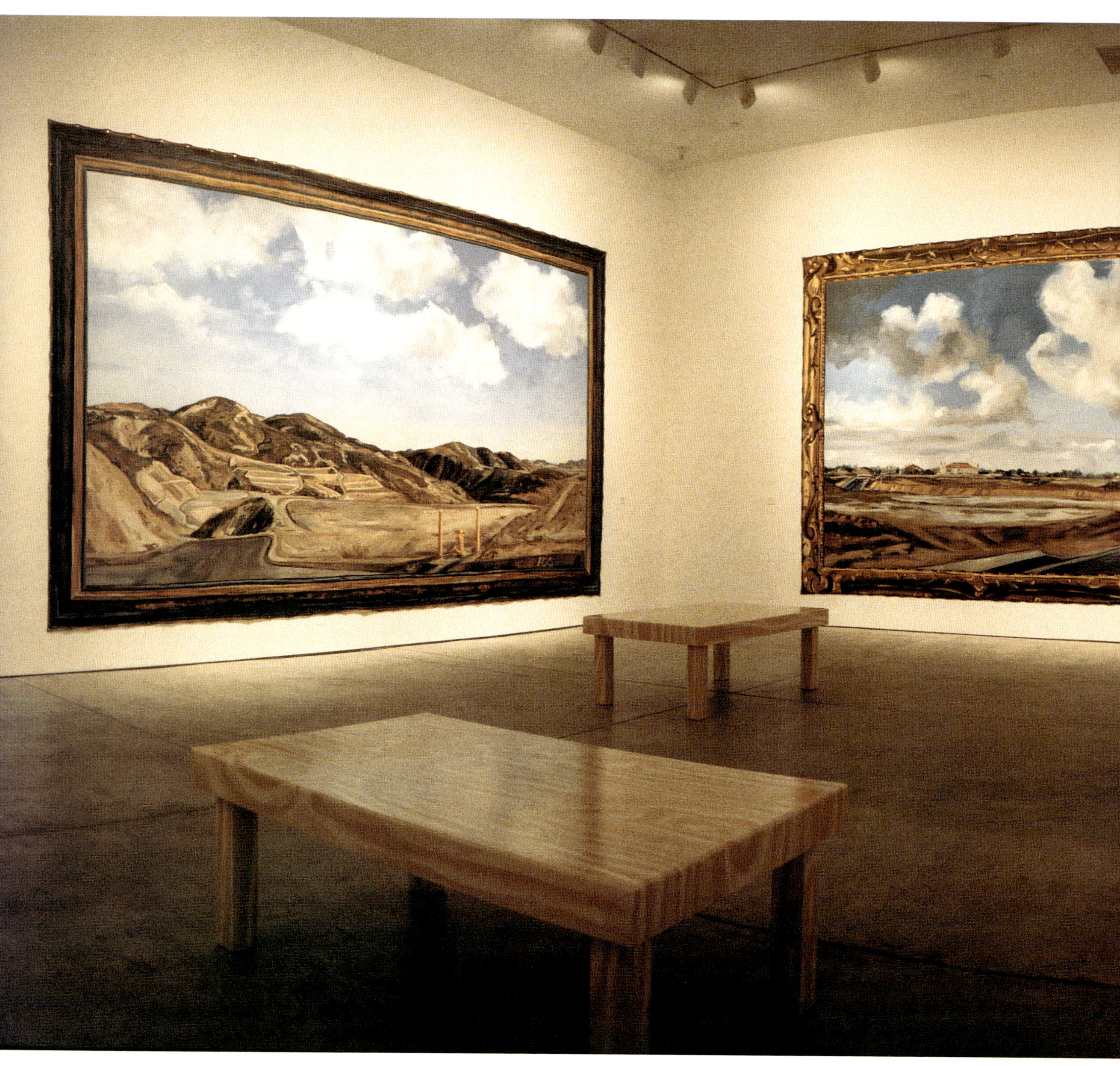

Installation view with **Rancho Cielo, Sienna Estates,** and **View from Laurentian St.,** 2000, Museum of Contemporary Art, San Diego

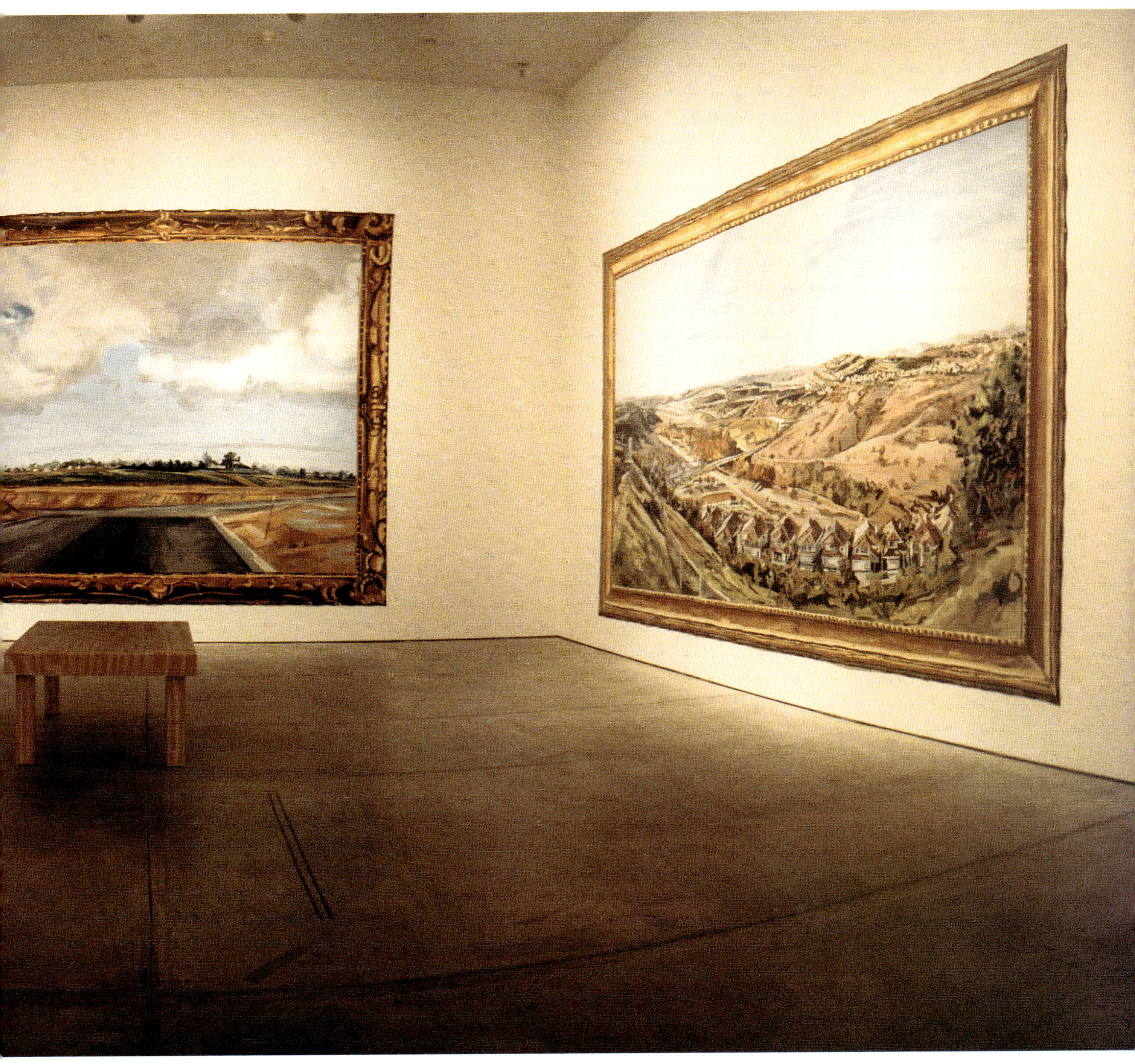

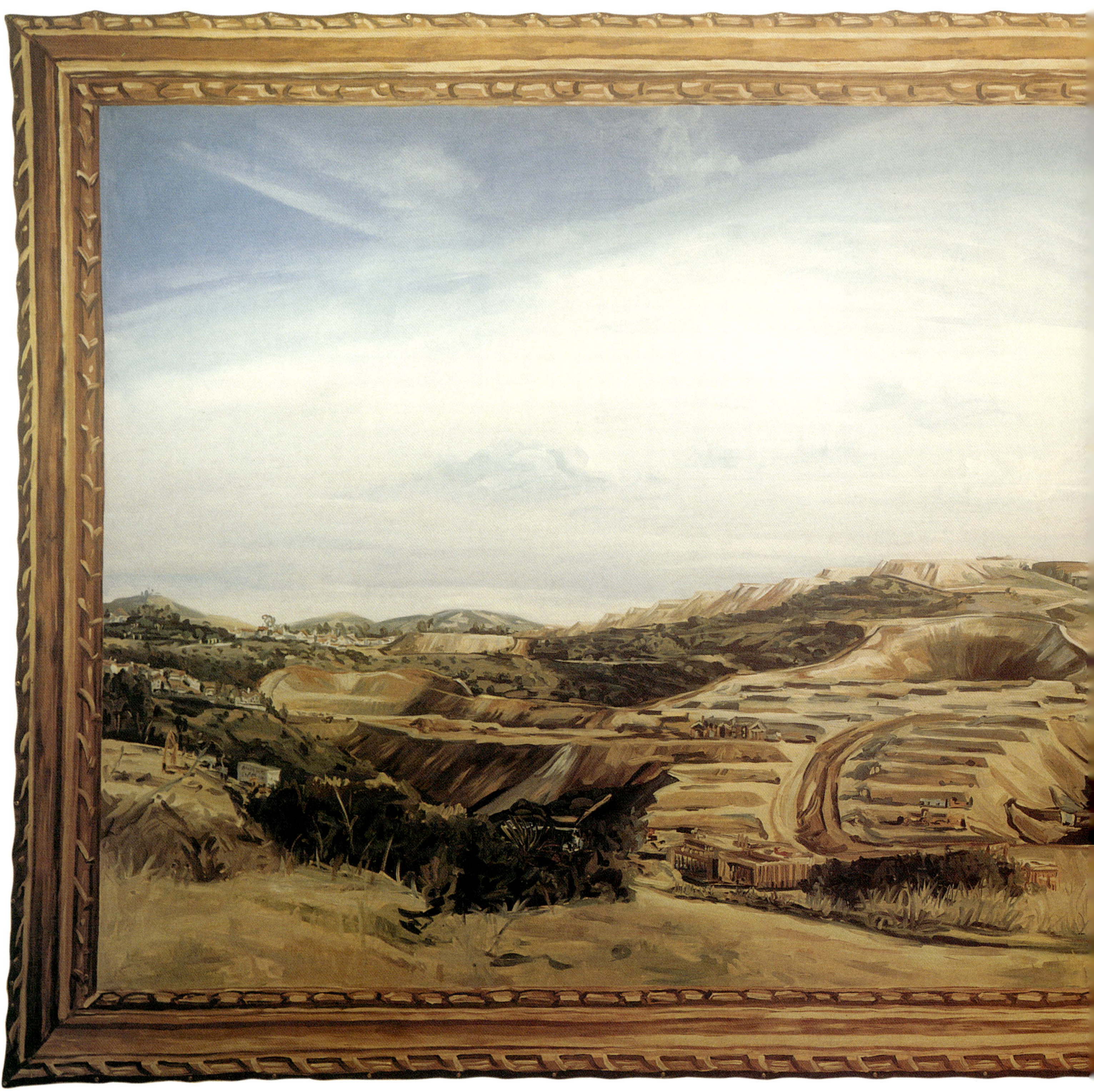

Rancho Dorado, 2000

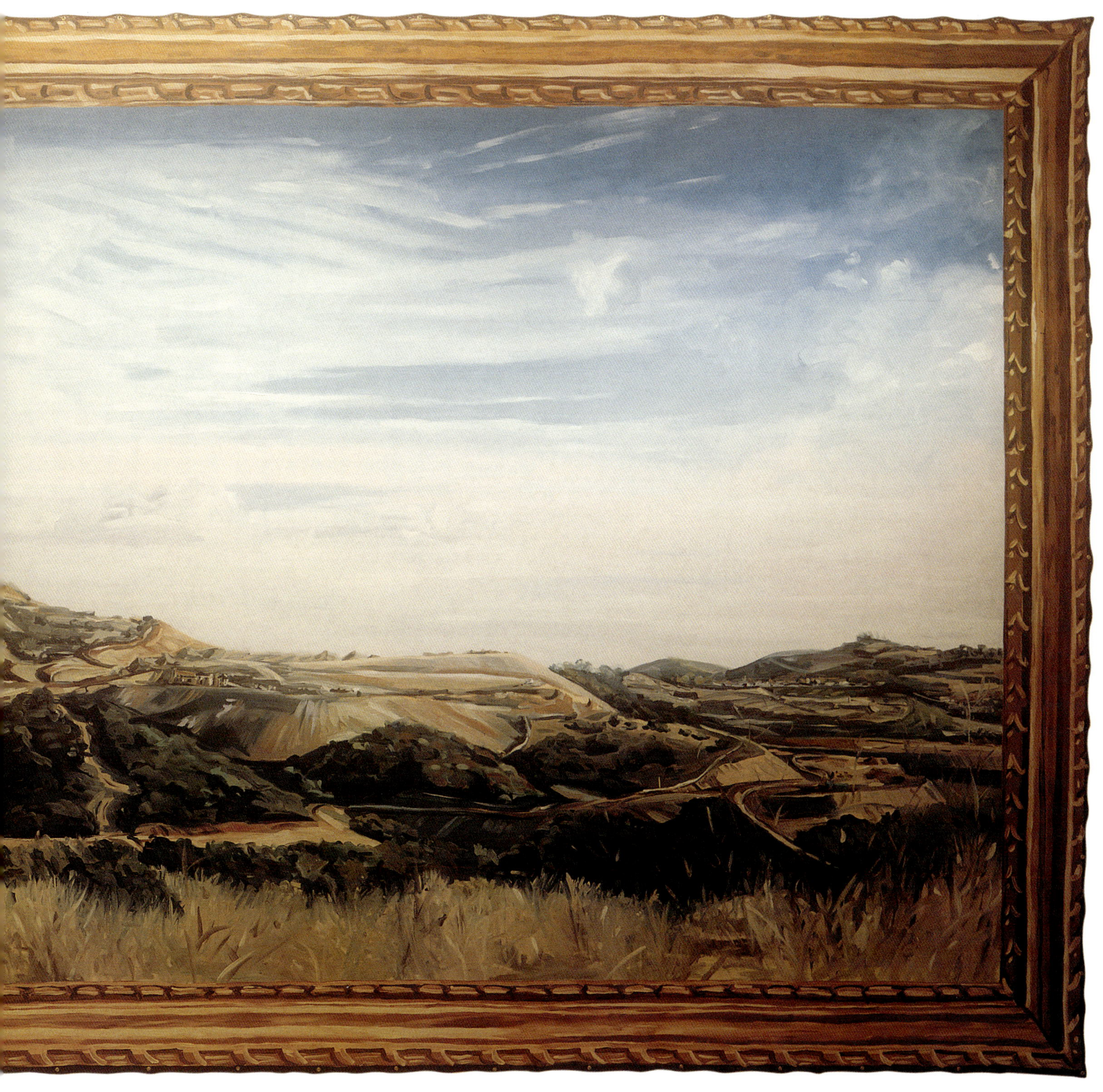

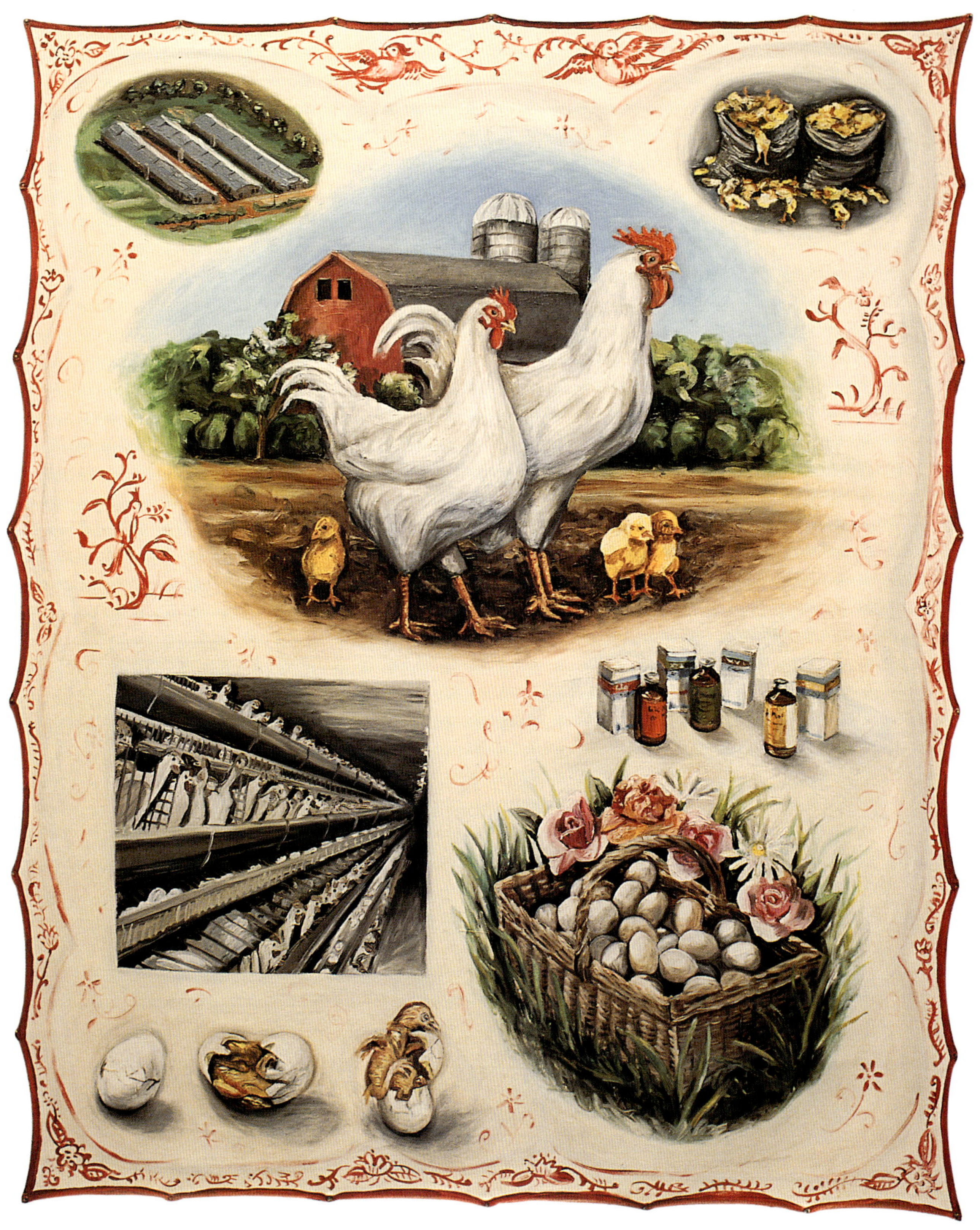

Egg Story, 1988

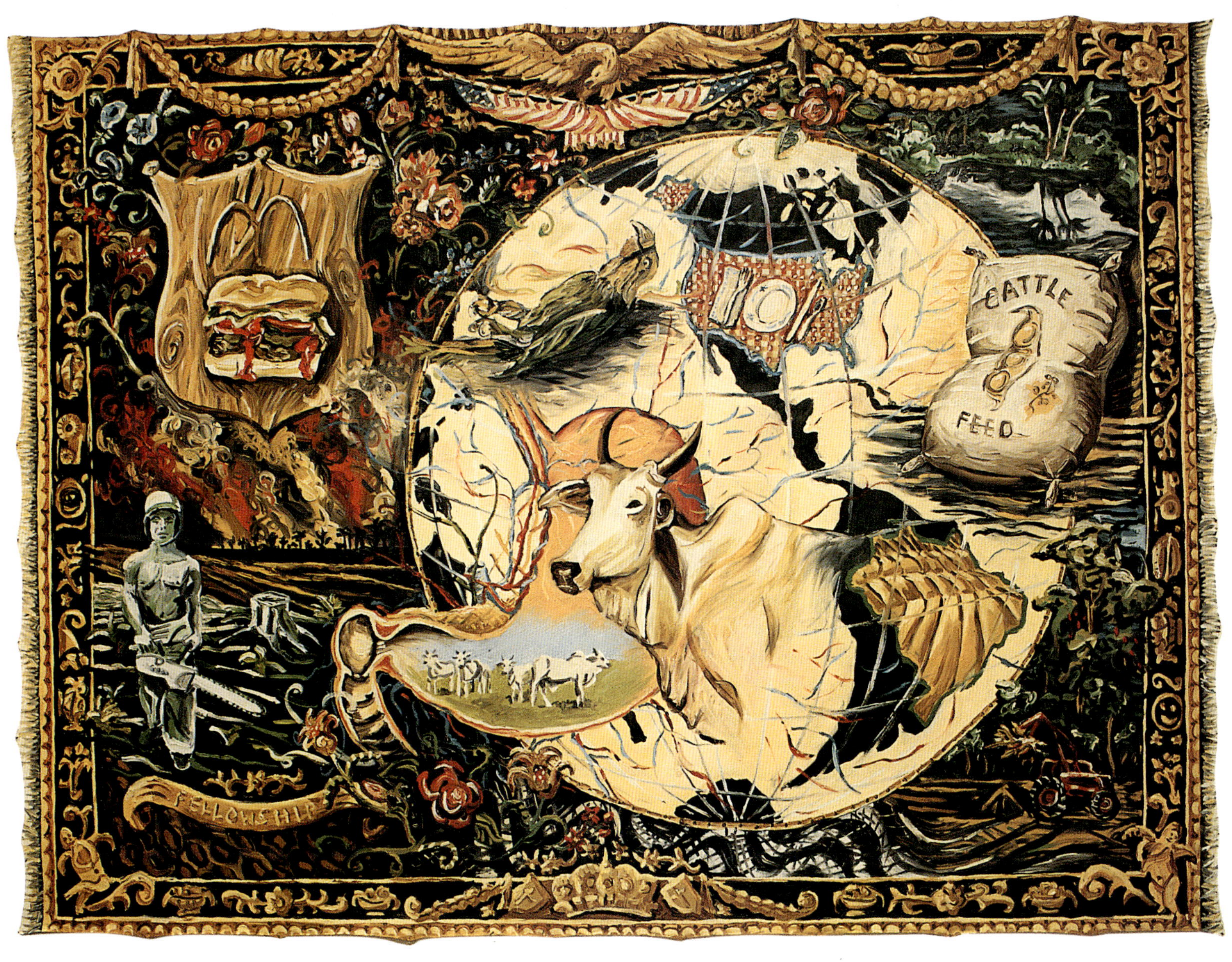



Supply Story, 1989

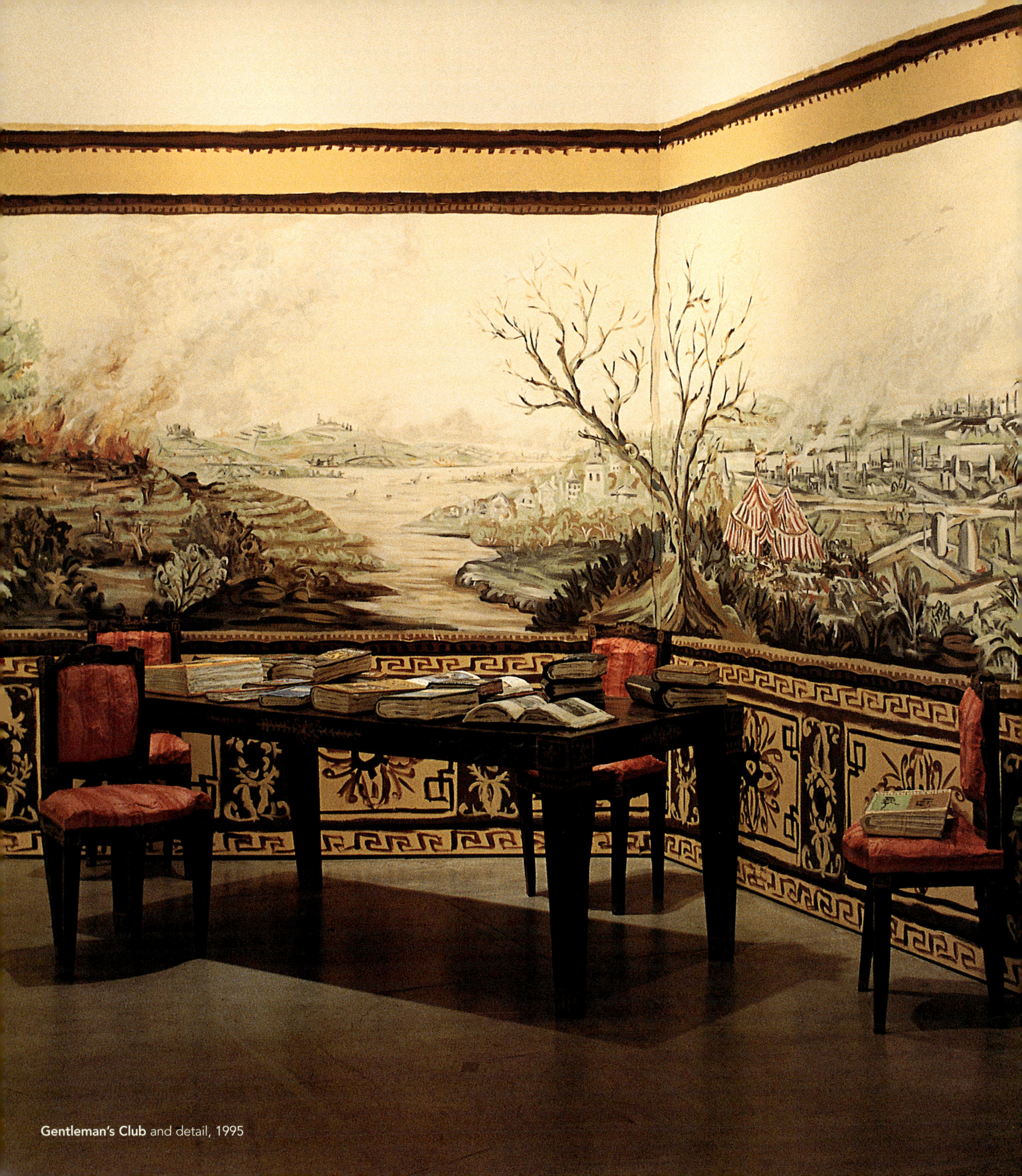


Gentleman's Club and detail, 1995

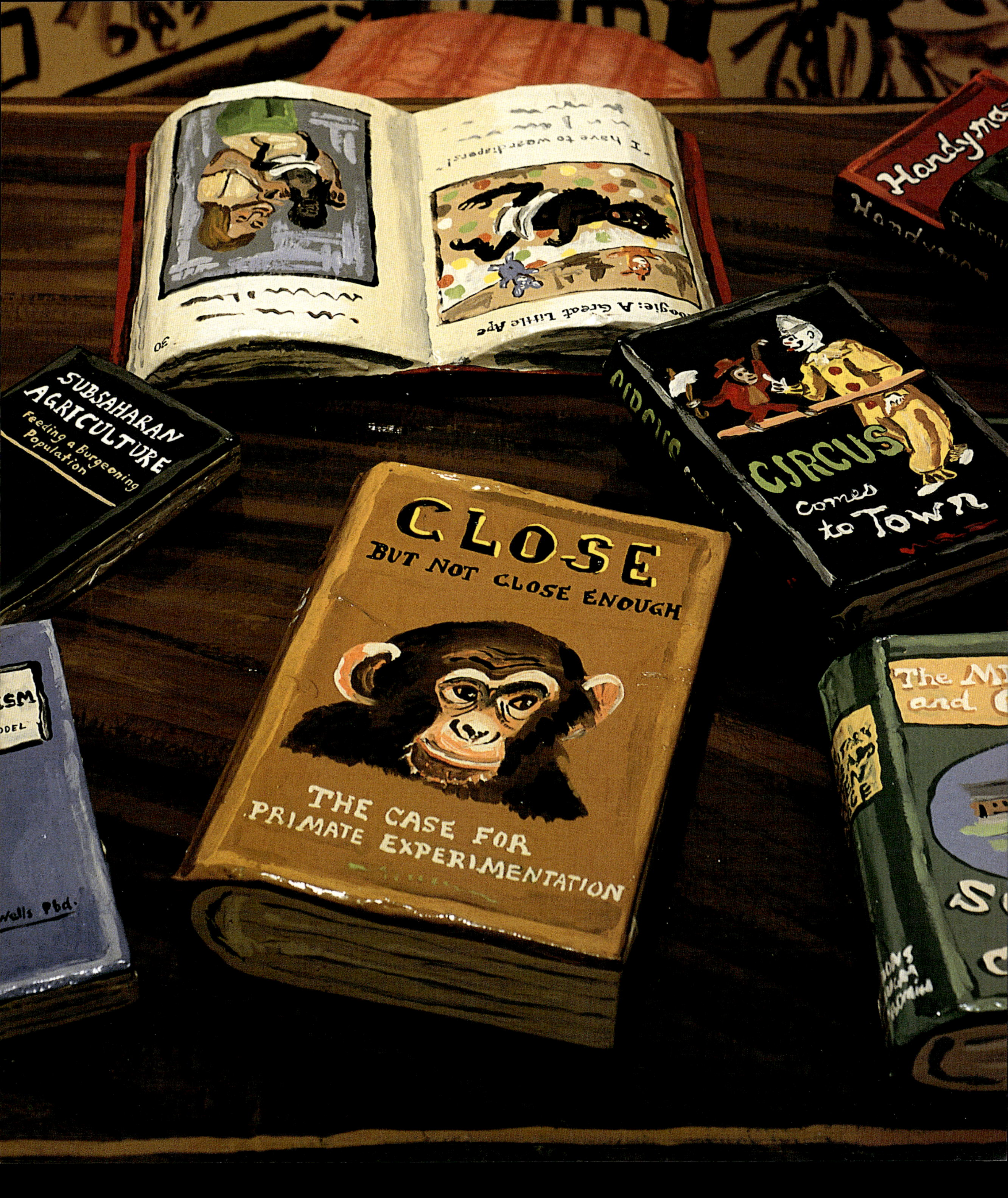
SUBSAHARAN AGRICULTURE
Feeding a Burgeoning Population
CLOSE
BUT NOT CLOSE ENOUGH
THE CASE FOR
PRIMATE EXPERIMENTATION
CIRCUS
comes to Town
Handyman
I have to wear diapers!
oogie: A Great Little Ape
Wells Pbd.
The M
and
30

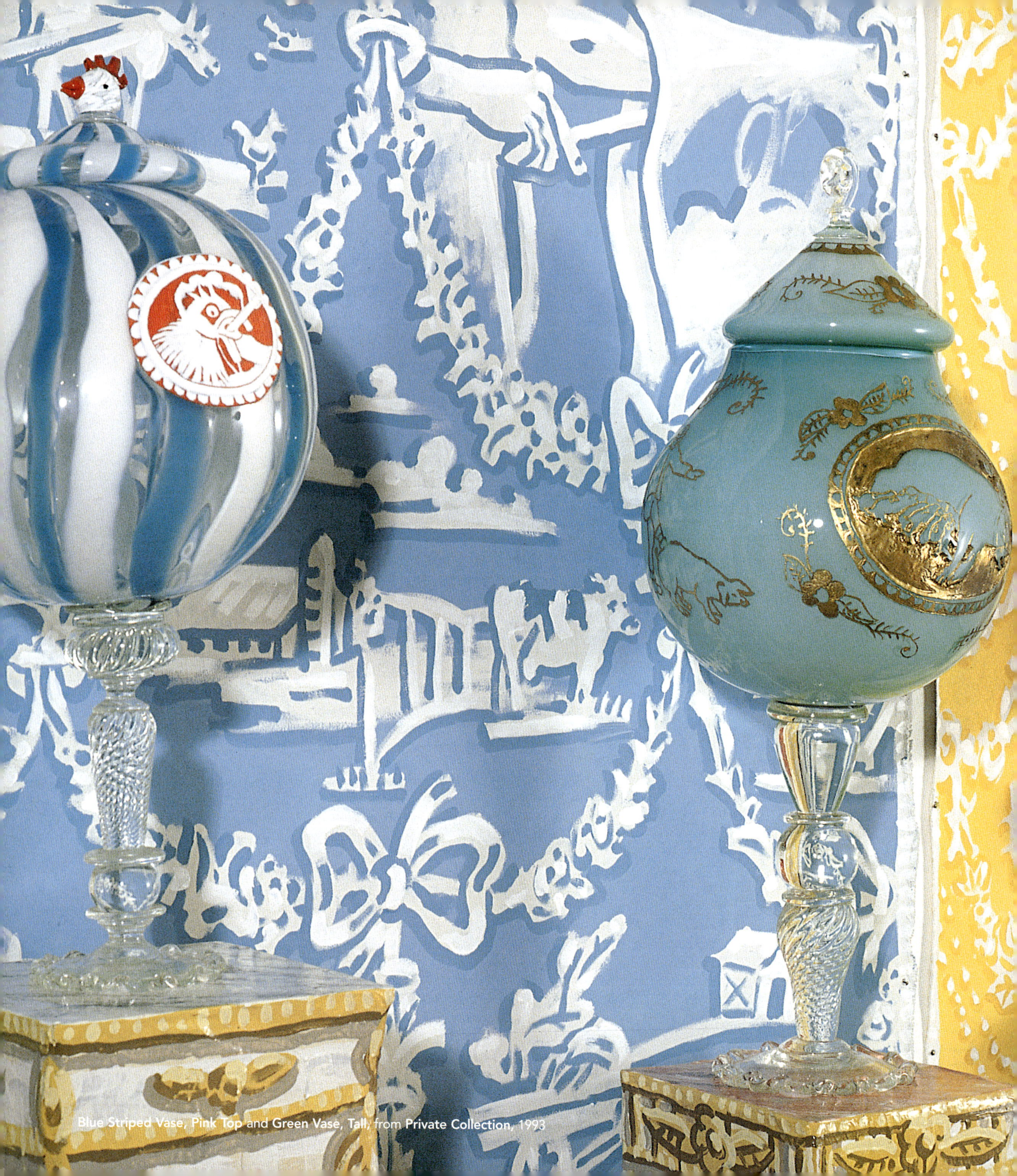

Blue Striped Vase, Pink Top and Green Vase, Tall, from Private Collection, 1993

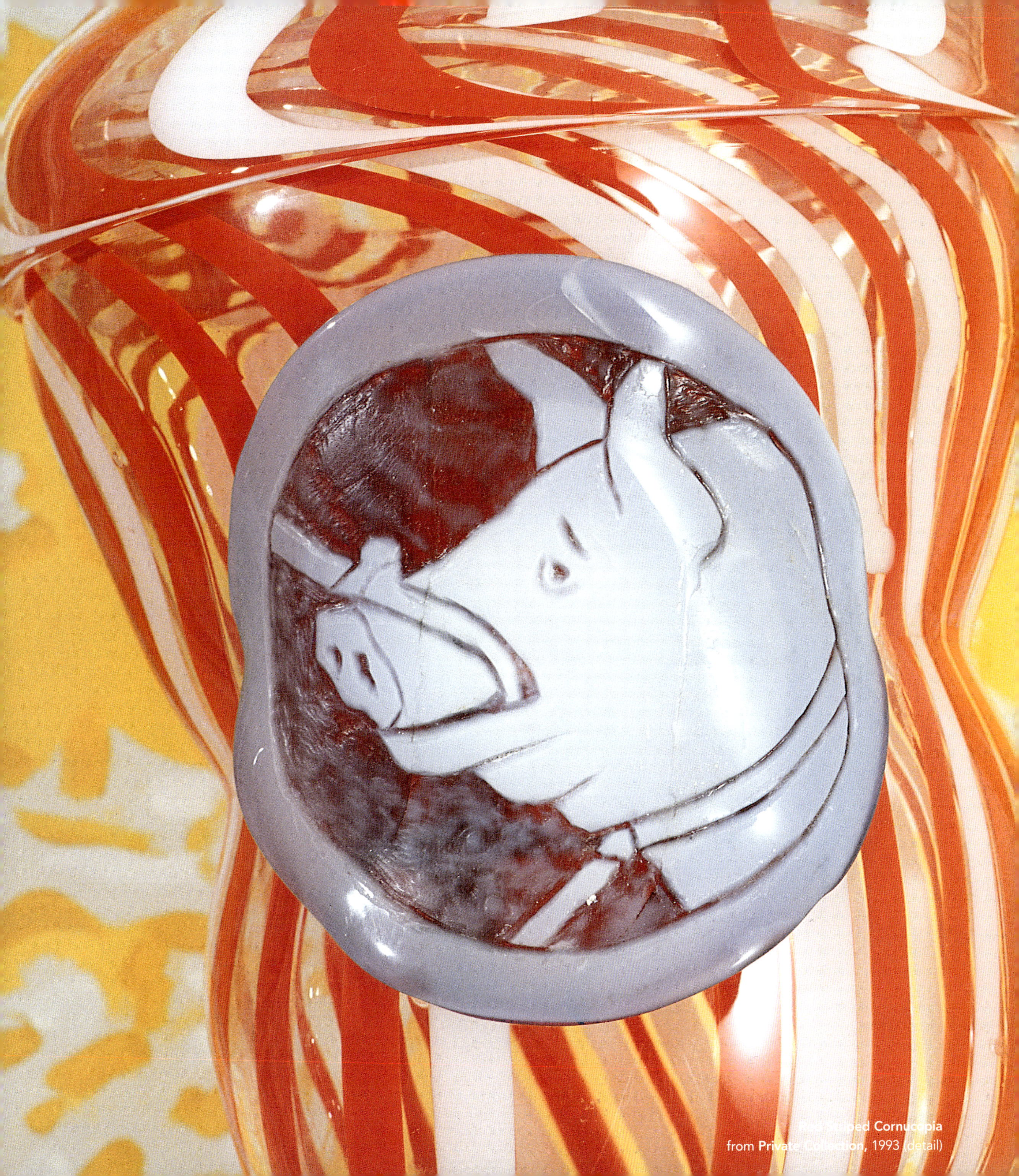

Pop Shaped Cornucopia
from Private Collection, 1993 (detail)

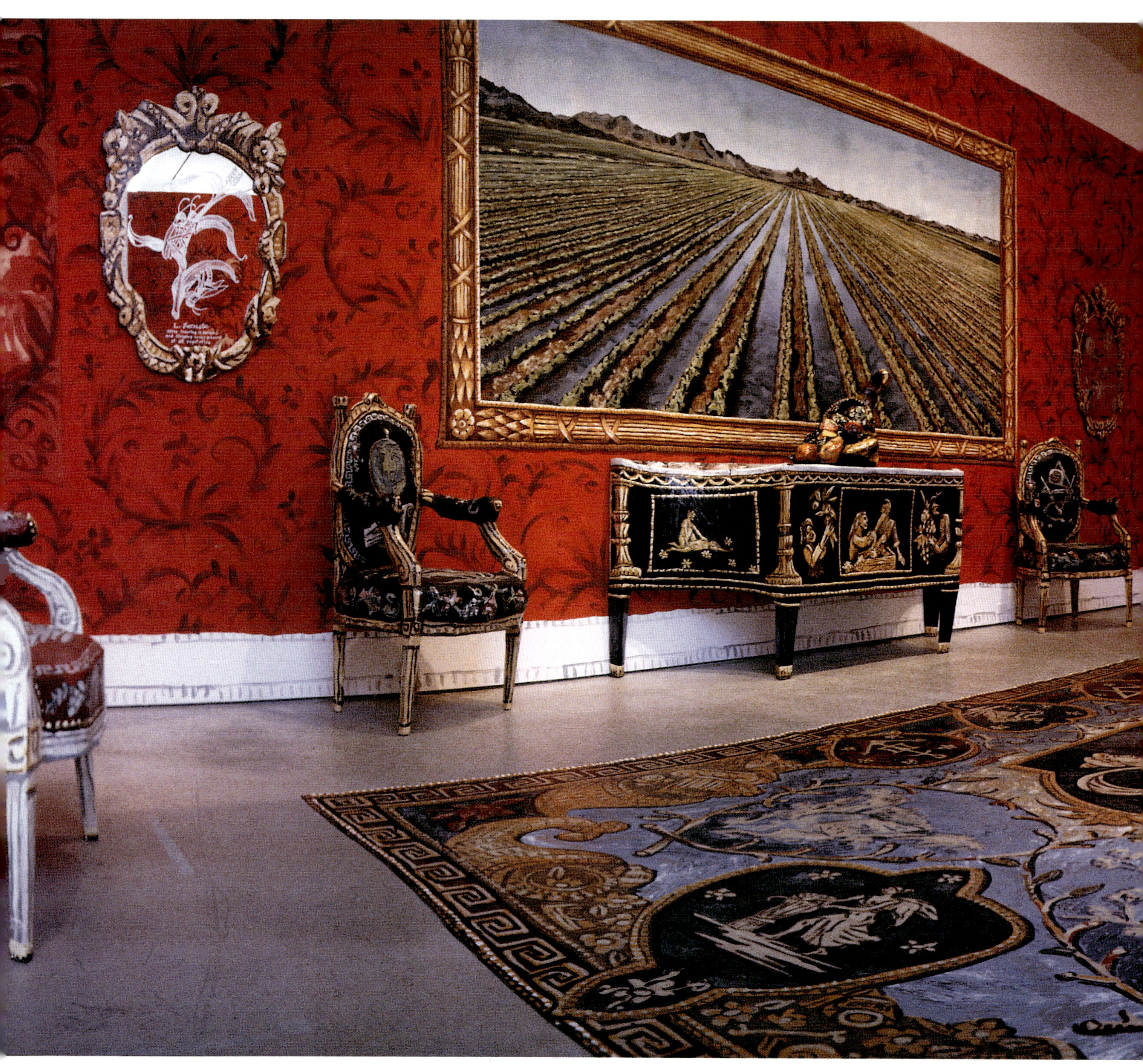

Accomplishments of Man, 1992–1993

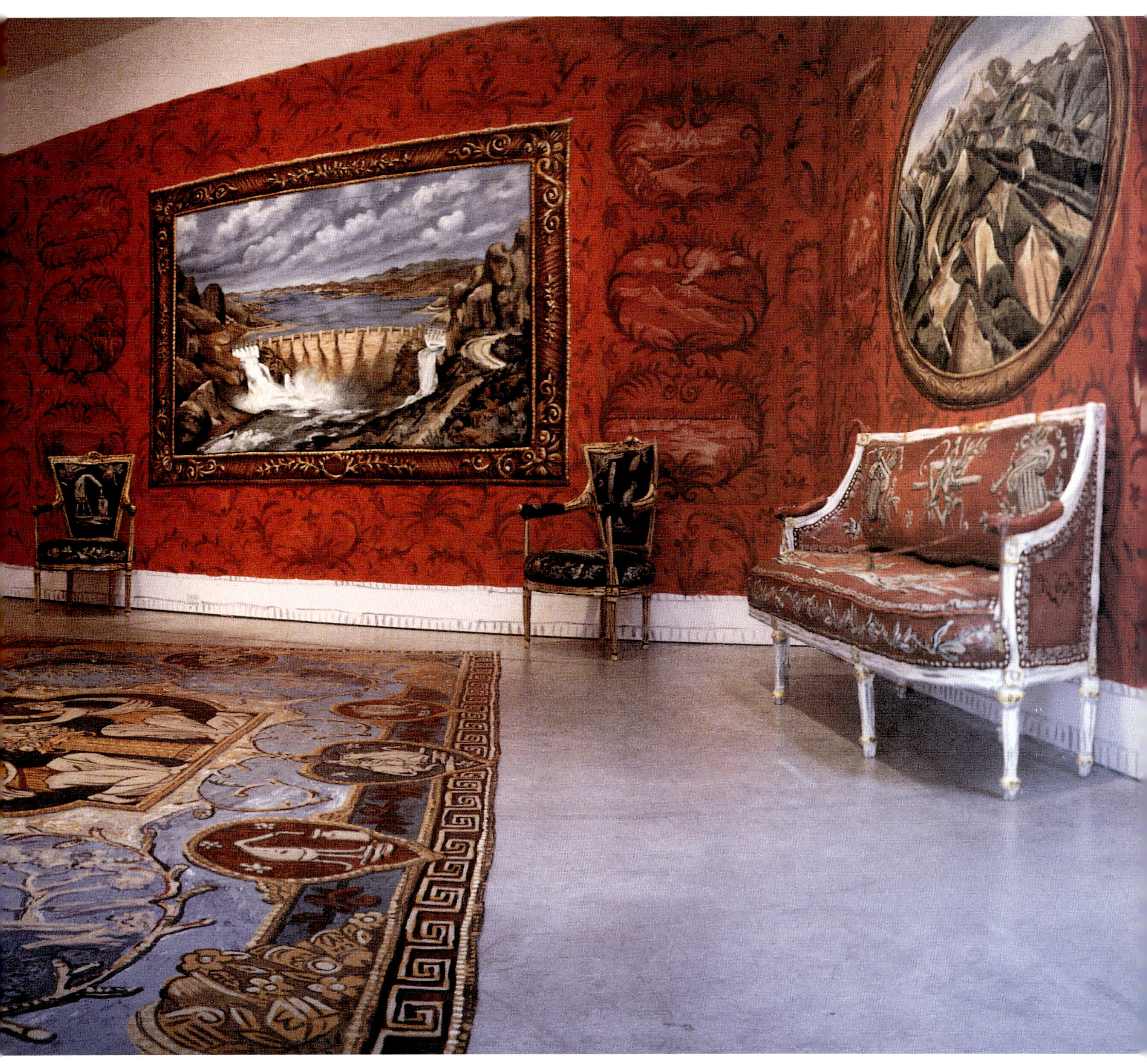

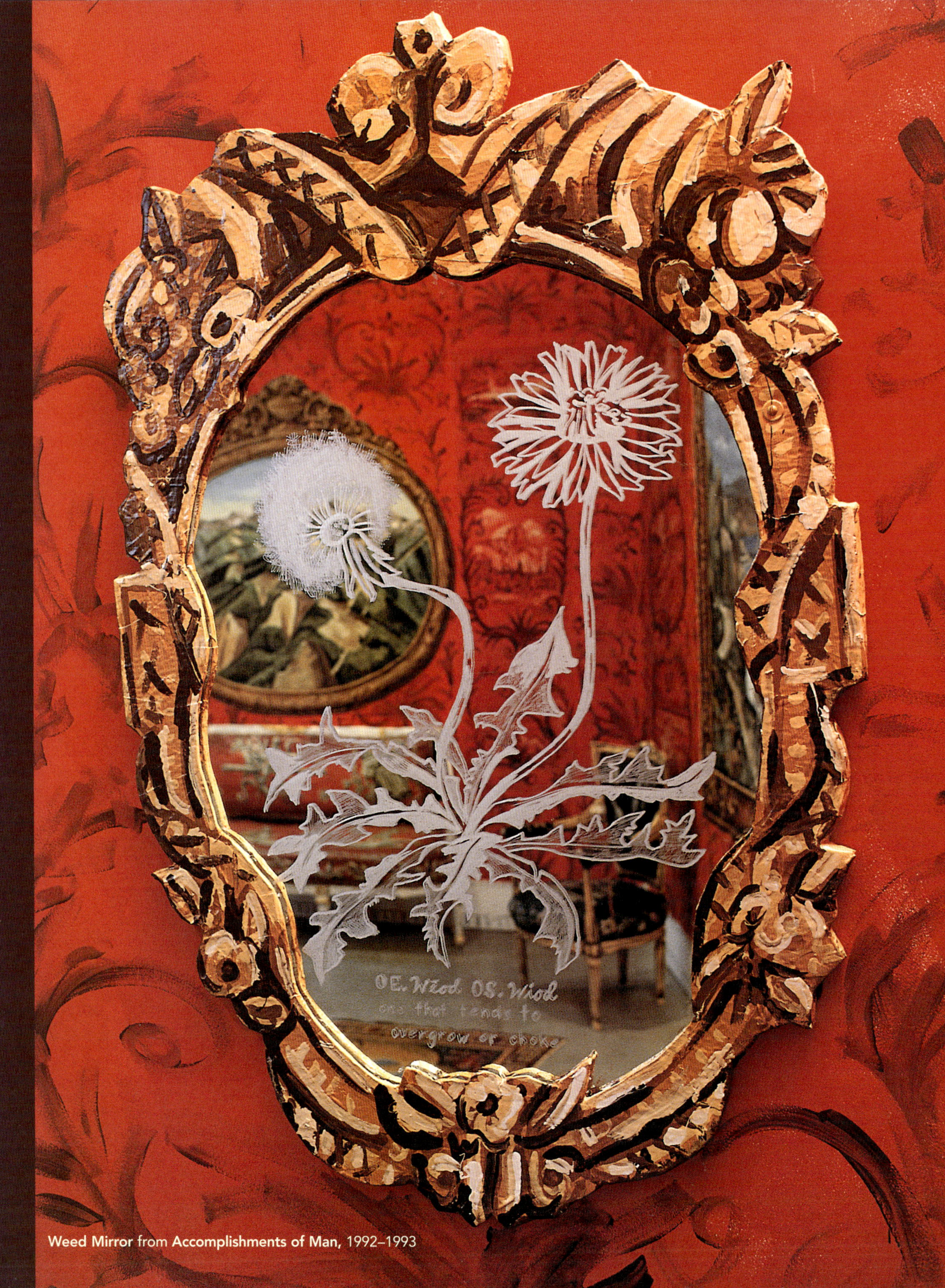


Weed Mirror from Accomplishments of Man, 1992–1993

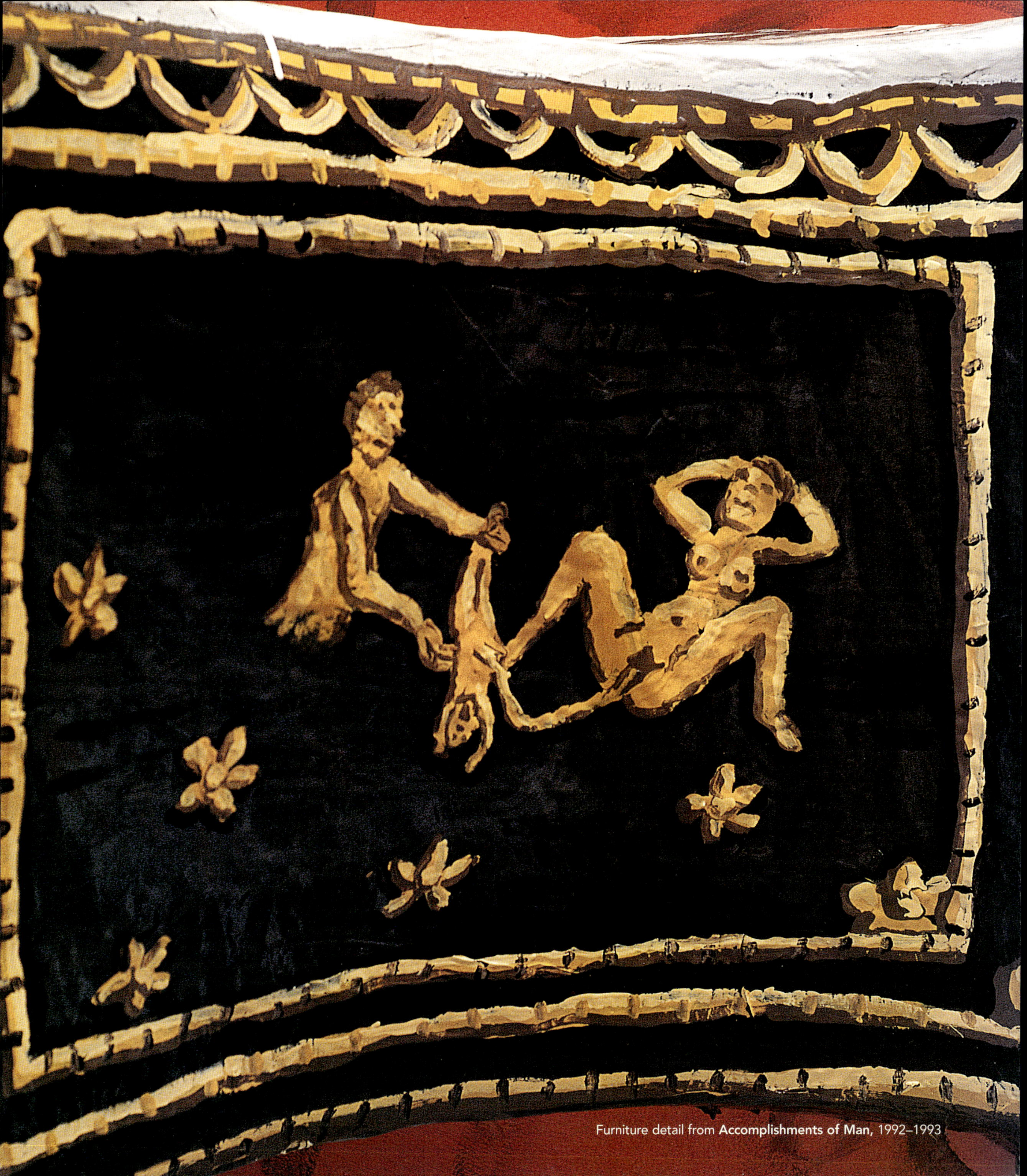

Furniture detail from **Accomplishments of Man**, 1992–1993

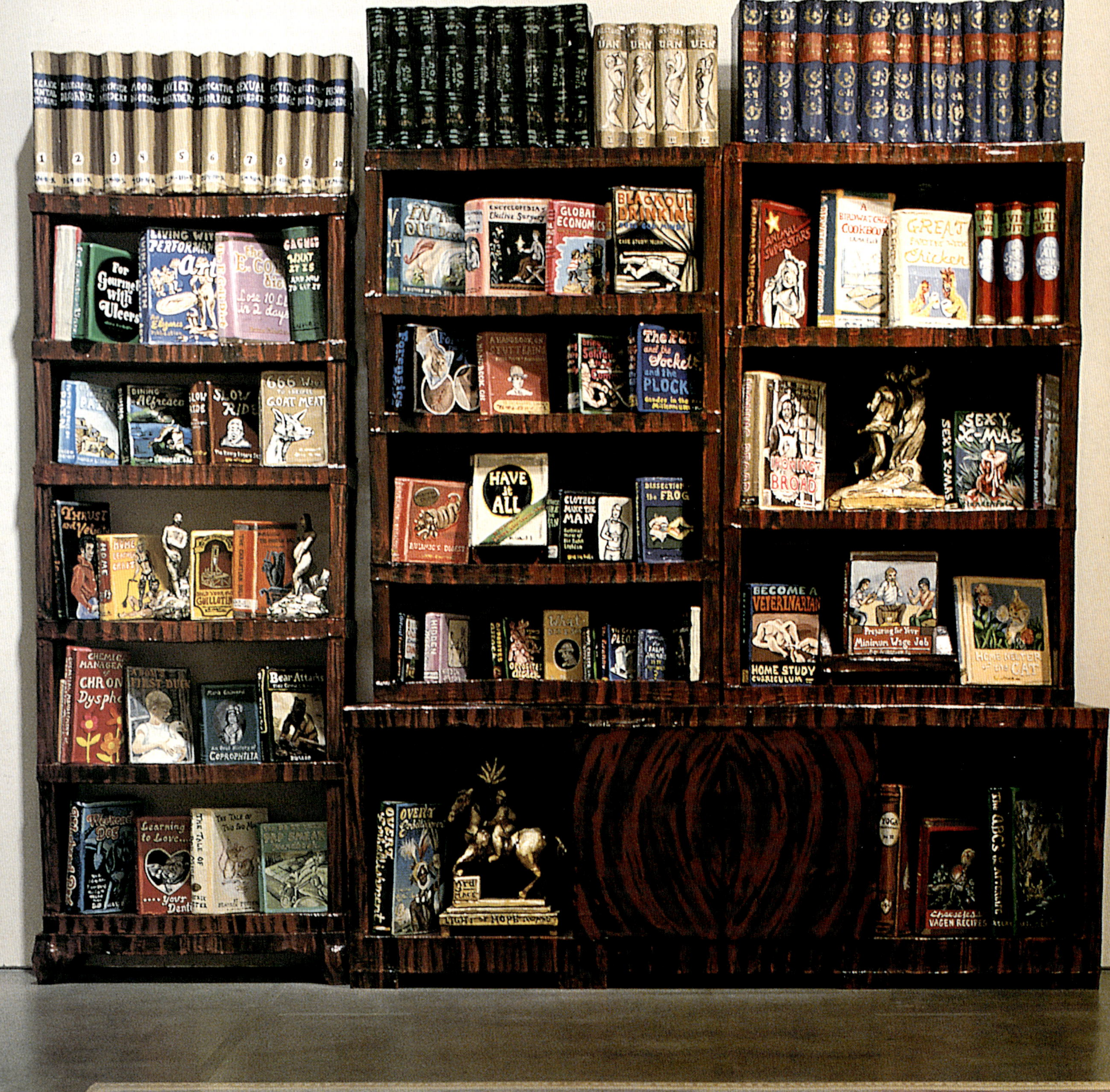

Selections from the Library of Dr. Pohatten
and detail, 1996–1999

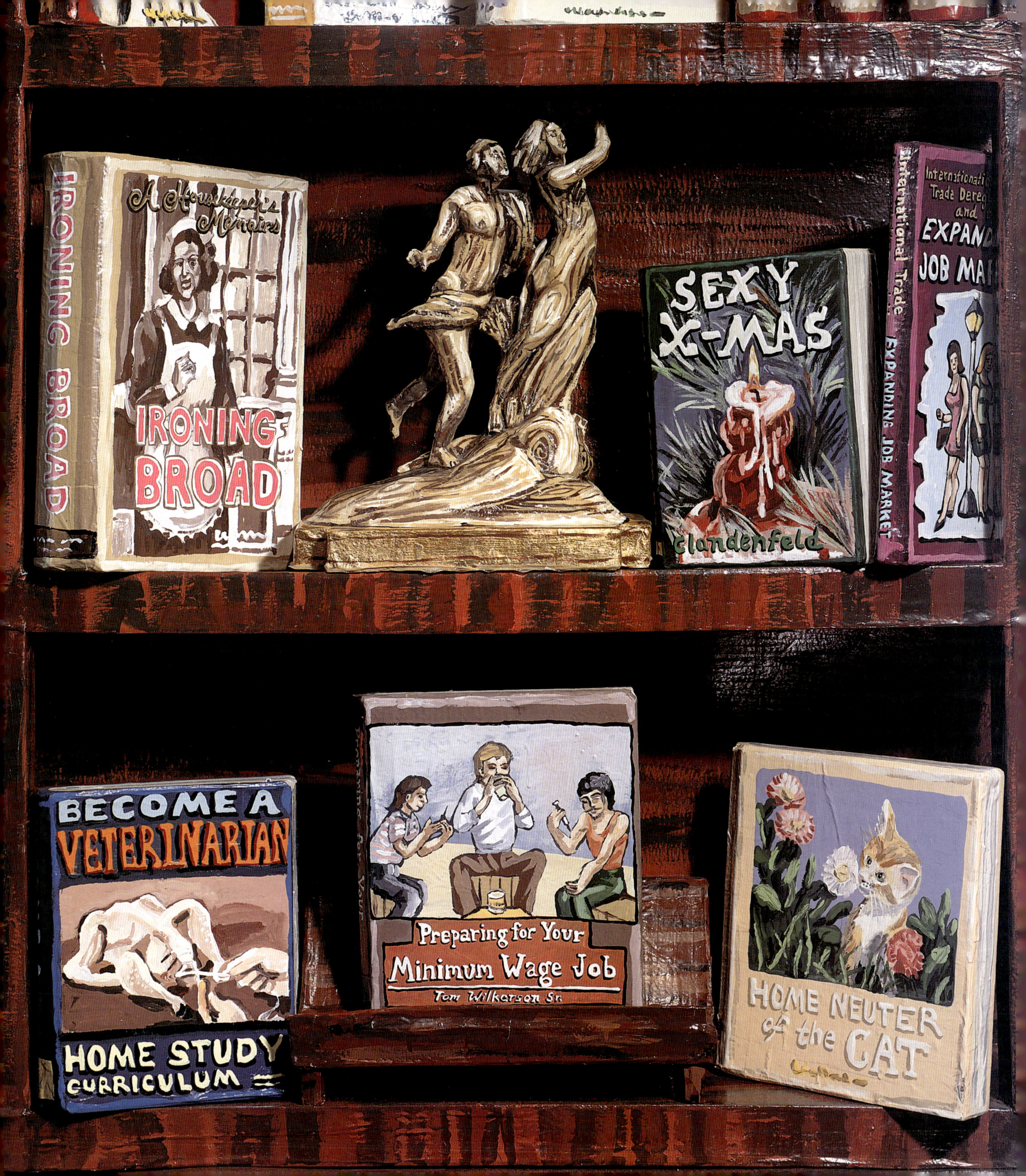

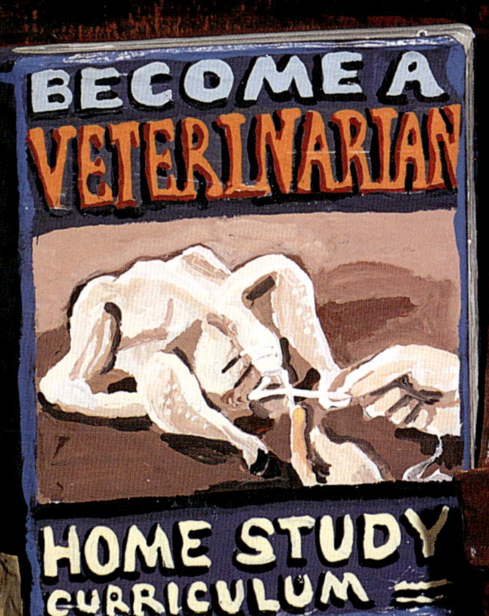

BECOME A
VETERINARIAN
HOME STUDY
CURRICULUM


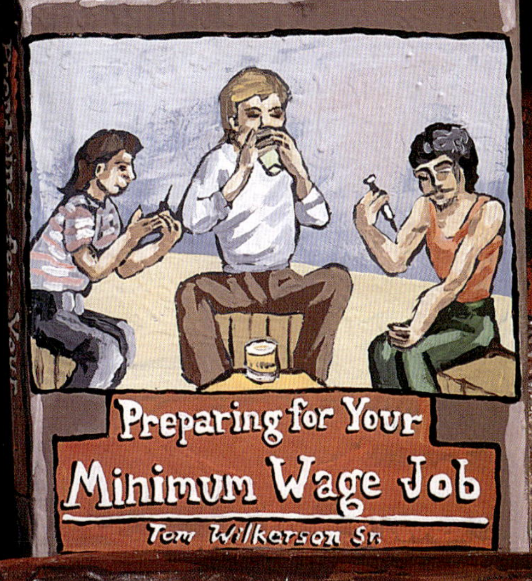

Preparing for Your
Minimum Wage Job
Tom Wilkerson Sr


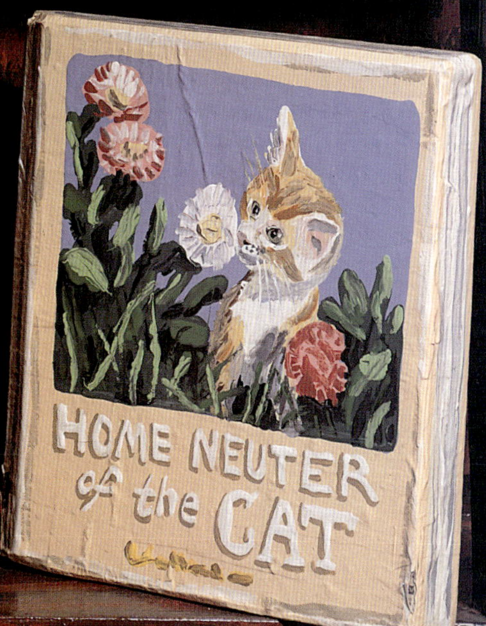

HOME NEUTER
of the CAT

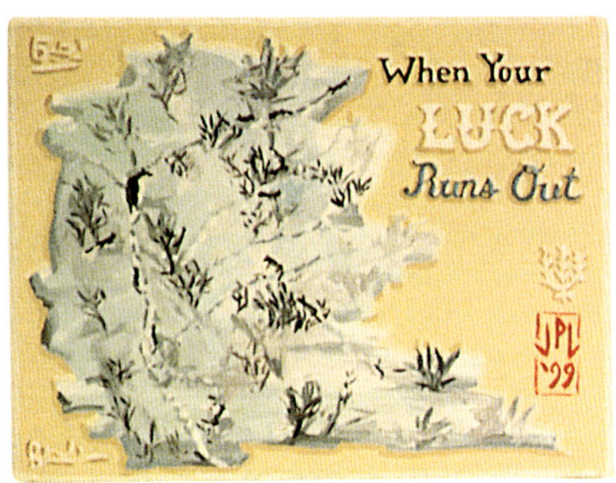


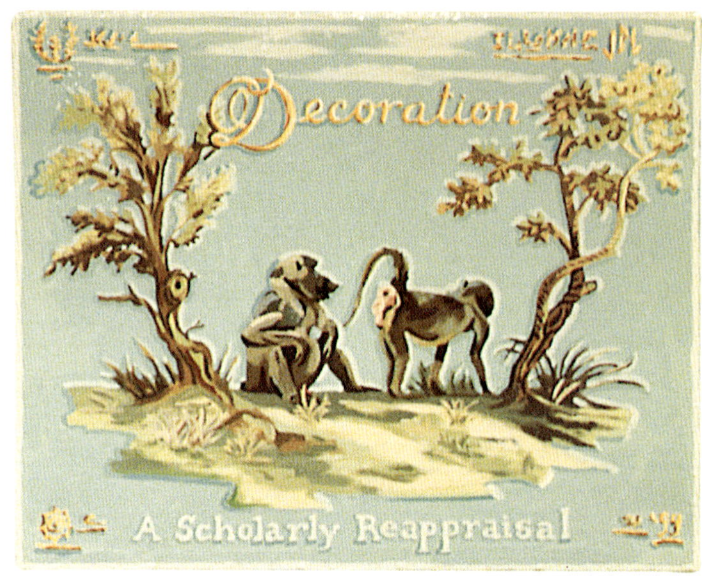


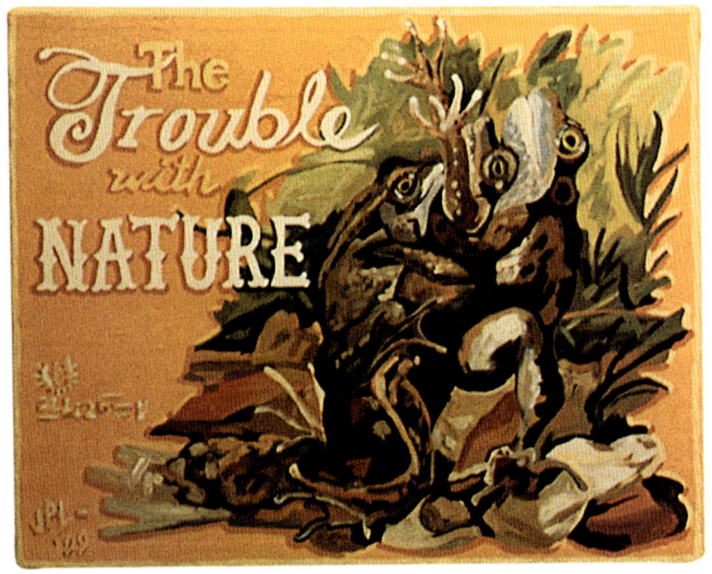


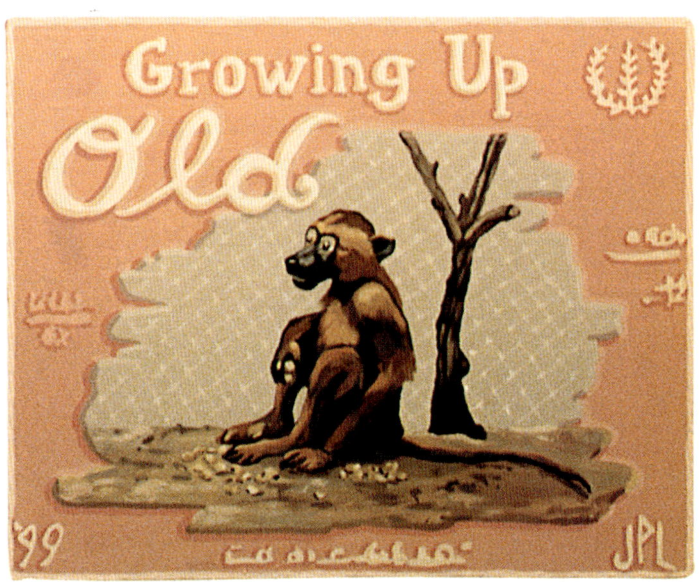


Panel paintings, 1999

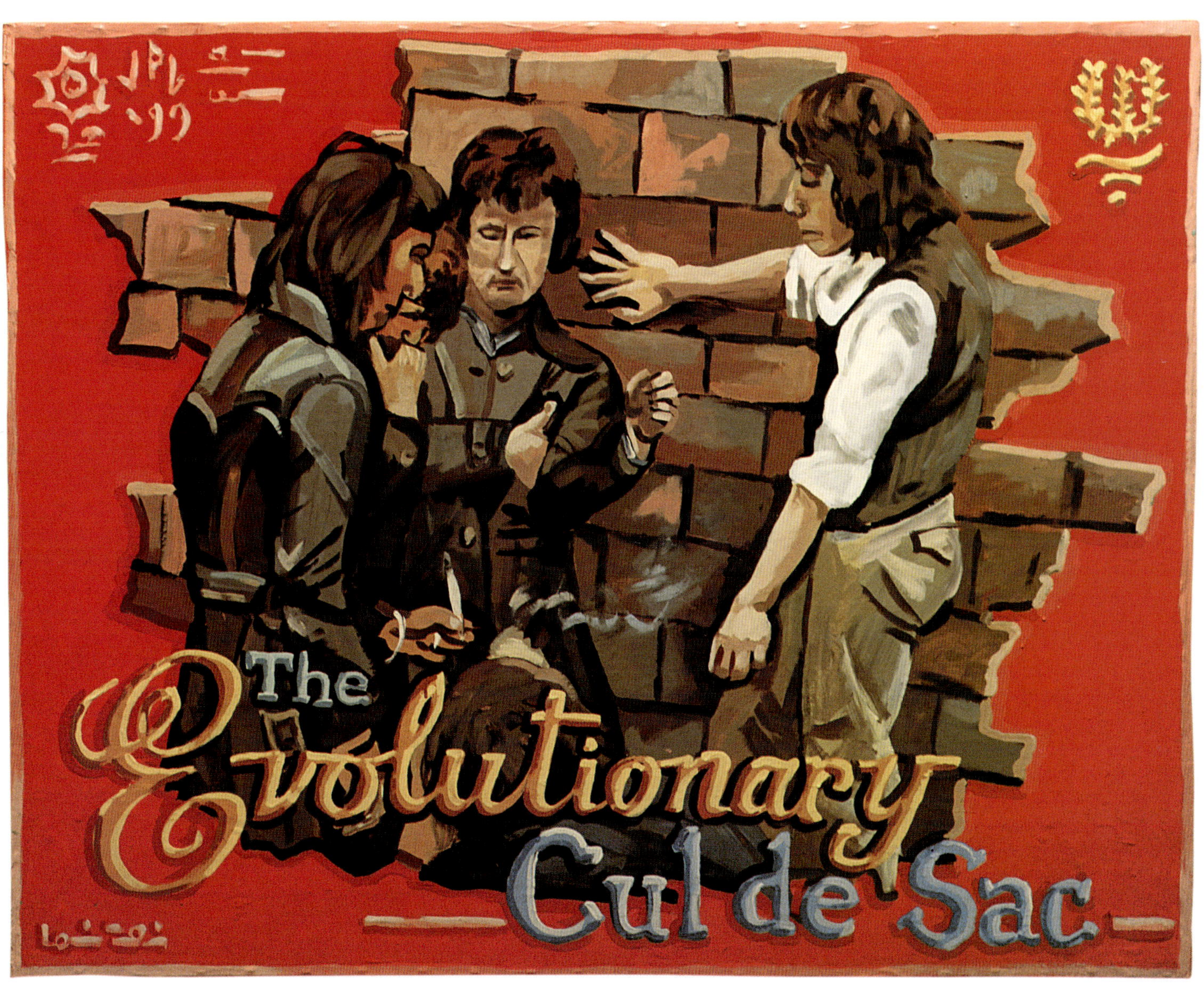

The
Evolutionary
Cul de Sac

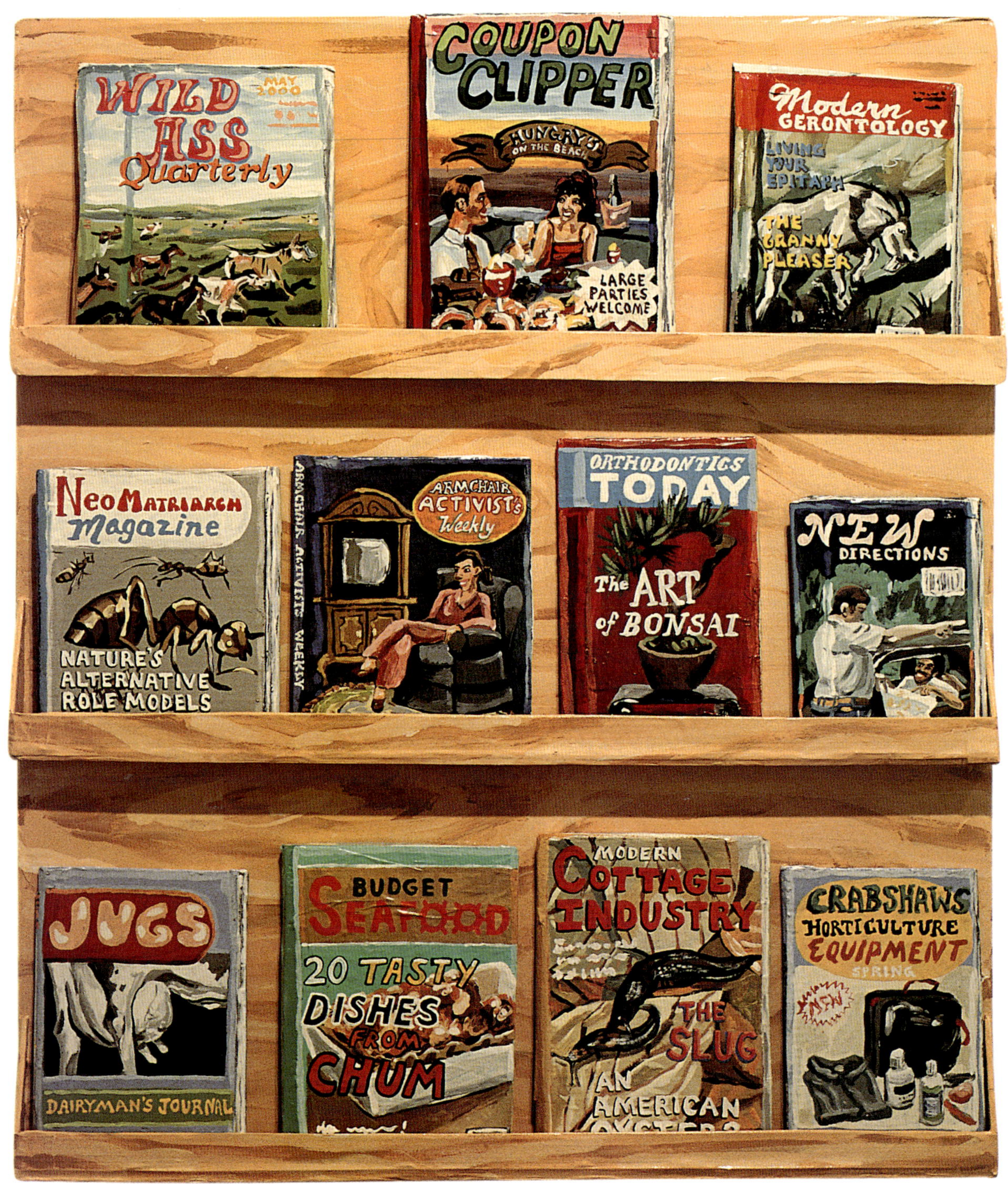


Magazine Rack, 1996–2000

# Exhibition Checklist

All works are Courtesy Quint Contemporary Art, La Jolla unless otherwise noted.
Dimensions are given in the following order: height, width, depth.

**Awards,** 1994–1996

SPCA, 1996
enamel and resin
on papier-mâché
25 x 32 x 2 inches

Diploma, 1994
enamel and resin
on papier-mâché
12 1/2 x 18 1/2 x 2 inches

First Place, 1994
enamel and resin
on papier-mâché
21 x 25 x 1/2 inches

Triple Trudgers, 1996
enamel and resin
on papier-mâché
1 x 14 x 1/2 inches

Memorandum, 1994
enamel and resin
on papier-mâché
13 x 18 x 2 inches

Outstanding Leadership, 1996
enamel and resin
on papier-mâché
21 x 28 x 2 inches

Magna cum Laude, 1996
enamel and resin
on papier-mâché
24 1/2 x 35 x 1 1/2 inches

Award, 1994
enamel and resin
on papier-mâché
21 x 28 x 2 inches

Recommendation, 1996
enamel and resin
on papier-mâché
24 1/2 x 28 x 2 inches

Lysol Urn, 1994
enamel, metal leaf, and resin
on papier-mâché
77 x 29 x 20 inches

Sienna Estates, 2000
oil on canvas
144 x 312 inches

View from Laurentian St., 2000
oil on canvas
120 x 216 inches

Rancho Dorado, 2000
oil on canvas
144 x 312 inches
Collection Museum of
Contemporary Art, San Diego
Gift of The Alberta duPont
Bonsal Foundation

Rancho Cielo, 2000
oil on canvas
144 x 252 inches

Bouquet, 2000
enamel, gold leaf, and resin
on papier-mâché and cloth
86 x 73 x 44 inches

Looking Good, 2000
etched mirror, enamel,
and wood
91 x 36 inches

Magazine Rack, 1996–2000
enamel on papier-mâché
47 x 43 x 4 inches

Coors Urn, 1994
enamel, metal leaf, and resin
on papier-mâché
77 x 24 x 24 inches

**Accomplishments of Man**
1992–1993

Desert Reclaimed, 1992
oil on canvas
84 x 170 inches

An Inland Sea, 1992–1993
oil on canvas
85 x 129 inches
Collection Museum of
Contemporary Art, San Diego
Museum purchase with funds
from the Elizabeth W. Russell
Foundation

The Renewable Resource, 1993
oil on canvas
78 x 85 inches

Weed Mirror, 1993/2000
etched mirror, papier-mâché,
enamel, wood
46 x 35 x 1 inch

Locust Mirror, 1993/2000
etched mirror, papier-mâché,
enamel, wood
46 x 31 x 1 inch

Crown Mirror, 1993
etched mirror, papier-mâché,
enamel, wood
53 x 40 inches

Cornucopia Rug, 1993
enamel on canvas
117 x 210 inches

various papier-mâché furniture,
wallpaper sections, and
site-specific painting

The Evolutionary Cul-de-Sac,
1999
enamel on papier-mâché
47 1/2 x 60 inches

The Trouble with Nature, 1999
enamel on papier-mâché
47 1/2 x 60 inches

Decoration, 1999
enamel on papier-mâché
47 1/2 x 60 inches

Growing Up Old, 1999
enamel on papier-mâché
47 1/2 x 60 inches

Country Lanes, 1999
enamel on papier-mâché
36 x 84 inches

Boy Power, 1999
enamel on papier-mâché
36 x 84 inches

Feminine Mystique, 1999
enamel on papier-mâché
36 x 84 inches

When Your Luck Runs Out, 1999
enamel on papier-mâché
36 x 84 inches

The Honor System's Grey Area,
2000
enamel on papier-mâché
36 x 84 inches

Flower Rug, 2000
enamel on canvas
120 x 168 inches

Selections from the Library of
Dr. Pohatten, 1996–1999
enamel on papier-mâché
117 x 124 x 17 inches

**Private Collection,** 1993/2000

Red Striped Cornucopia,
Green Top, 1993
etched and blown glass,
papier-mâché, wood, enamel
30 x 11 x 11 inches;
41 1/2 x 12 x 12 inches

Green Vase, Tall, 1993
etched and blown glass,
papier-mâché, wood, enamel
35 x 14 x 14 inches;
48 x 11 1/2 x 11 1/2 inches

Blue Striped Vase, Pink Top,
1993
etched and blown glass,
papier-mâché, wood, enamel
29 x 23 x 14 inches;
41 1/2 x 11 x 11 inches

Wallpaper, 1993/2000
acrylic on canvas (2 pieces)
102 x 56 1/2 inches; 102 x 36 inches

Gentlemen's Club, 1995
painting on canvas, site–specific
painting, papier-mâché and
enamel objects
dimensions variable

Supply Story, 1989
oil on canvas
85 x 115 inches
Collection of Dietrich Jenny

Coverlet, 1989
oil on canvas
103 x 95 1/2 inches
Collection of Dietrich Jenny

Post-Colonial Divan, 1990
found furniture, acrylic on canvas,
enamel, fabric
32 x 101 x 111 inches

Mean Spirited Floor Covering, 1990
enamel on canvas, latex
118 x 106 inches

Egg Story, 1988
oil on canvas
68 x 54 inches
The Bodi Collection

Wallpaper Sample, 1987
oil on canvas
71 x 52 inches
The Bodi Collection

The Integument, 1987
oil on canvas
72 x 60 inches
The Bodi Collection

Petroleum Story, 1988
oil on canvas
72 x 60 inches
Collection of Dietrich Jenny

Personal Care Products, 1994
papier-mâché, enamel,
metal leaf, resin
dimensions variable

The Loneliness Clinic, 1996
enamel on papier-mâché
27 x 28 inches
Collection Max and
Melissa Elliott

# Biography

Born 1960 in Eureka, California
Resides in Encinitas, California

## Education

**1988**
Master of Fine Arts, University of California, San Diego

**1983**
Bachelor of Arts, University of California, Berkeley

## Professional Position

**1992-Present**
Visiting Lecturer, University of California, San Diego

## Select Awards

**2000**
Grant, The Alberta duPont Bonsal Foundation

**1993**
Western States Arts Federation/National Endowment
for the Arts Regional Fellowship

**1992**
Fellowship, Art Matters, Inc., New York, New York
Grant, California Arts Council
Grant, Culture and Animals Foundation

**1991**
Western States Arts Federation/National Endowment
for the Arts Regional Fellowship
Grant, Pollock-Krasner Foundation, New York, New York

## Selected Solo Exhibitions

• catalogue or brochure

**2000**
Jean Lowe: The Evolutionary Cul-de-Sac
Museum of Contemporary Art, San Diego •

Books and Ideas in an Age of Anxiety: Selections from the Annex,
Athenaeum, La Jolla, California

**1999**
Zoo Story (collaboration with Kim MacConnel),
University Art Gallery, University of California, San Diego

**1998**
Cat's Cradle, Galerie Françoise et ses frères,
Lutherville, Maryland

In the Eddy of Manifest Destiny, Quint Contemporary Art,
La Jolla, California

**1997**
Dr. Pohatten's, Holly Solomon Gallery, New York, New York

**1996**
Pomp and Circumstance, Holly Solomon Gallery,
New York, New York; Galerie Françoise et ses frères,
Lutherville, Maryland

How To Win At Scratchers, Quint Contemporary Art,
La Jolla, California

Accomplishments of Man, The Contemporary Arts Center,
Cincinnati, Ohio

**1995**
Bull Story (collaboration with Kim MacConnel),
Holly Solomon Gallery, New York, New York

Accomplishments of Man, California Center for the Arts Museum,
Escondido, California •

**1994**
Domestic Space, Gracie Mansion Fine Arts,
New York, New York

Galerie van Mourik, Rotterdam, The Netherlands •

Real Nature: Accomplishments of Man,
Madison Center for the Arts, Madison, Wisconsin •

A Lesson in Civics, inSITE94, Casa de la Cultura,
Tijuana, Baja California, Mexico •

**1993**

Lost Nature, Quint Contemporary Art, La Jolla, California

Bull Story (collaboration with Kim MacConnel),
Museum of Contemporary Art, San Diego

Real Nature: Accomplishments of Man,
LACE (Los Angeles Contemporary Exhibitions),
Los Angeles, California

**1992**
Tale of the Bull/Cuento del Toro
(collaboration with Kim MacConnel),
Casa de la Cultura, Tijuana, Baja California, Mexico

Jardin Zoologique, Founders' Gallery,
University of San Diego, San Diego, California

**1990-1992**
A Dilettante's Conversation on the Topics of
Anthropocentrism and Western Consumerism,
Pittsburgh Center for the Arts, Pittsburgh, Pennsylvania; Hoffman
Gallery, Oregon School of Arts and Crafts, Portland, Oregon; Laguna
Art Museum Satellite at South Coast Plaza, Costa Mesa, California;
Gracie Mansion Fine Art, New York, New York

**1989**
Grand Plan, Southern Exposure Gallery,
San Francisco, California

Bad Boss Story, Gracie Mansion Fine Art,
New York, New York

**1988**
Dietrich Jenny Gallery, San Diego, California

Mandeville Annex Gallery, University of California, San Diego

**Selected Group Exhibitions**

• catalogue or brochure

**2000**
The Next Wave: New Painting in Southern California,
California Center for the Arts, Escondido, California •

New Voices, Delaware Art Museum, Delaware, Maryland

**1999**
Hollybury.usa, Mayor Gallery, London, United Kingdom

**1998**
Group Show, Quint Contemporary Art, La Jolla, California

**1997**
Animal Kingdom, New Jersey Center for Visual Arts,
Summit, New Jersey •

Sixteen Artists From California, California Rush,
Sag Harbor, New York

Group Show, Quint Contemporary Art, La Jolla, California

In Memory of Pleasure, Kohler Arts Center
Sheboygen, Wisconsin

**1996**
Anima Mundi, James Graham & Sons Gallery,
New York, New York

Home Show II, Santa Barbara Contemporary Arts Forum,
Santa Barbara, California •

Subversive Domesticity, Edwin A. Ulrich Museum,
Wichita, Kansas •

**1995**
Wallpaper Works, Contemporary Arts Museum,
Houston, Texas •

Next of Kin: Looking at the Great Apes,
MIT List Visual Arts Center, Cambridge, Massachusetts •

Going For Baroque, The Contemporary,
(at the Walters Art Gallery), Baltimore, Maryland •

Fun House, E.S. Vandam, New York, New York

Issues of Empire, Guggenheim Gallery,
Chapman University, Orange, California •

Group Exhibition, Quint Contemporary Art,
La Jolla, California

**1994**
Bad Girls West, Fisher Gallery
University of Southern California, Los Angeles •

Dancing Frogs and Altarwings: Animal Allegories
in Contemporary Art, Kohler Arts Center,
Sheboygan, Wisconsin

**1993**
Local Production/San Diego Area Artists,
California Center for the Arts, Escondido

From Destruction to Reclamation: Endangered Life, Southeastern
Center for Contemporary Art, Winston-Salem, North Carolina

U.S.A. Today in Fiber Art, Netherlands Textile Museum,
Tilburg, The Netherlands; Museum of Applied Arts, Helsinki, Finland •

**1992**
From the Studio: Recent Painting and Sculpture
by 20 California Artists, The Oakland Museum,
Oakland, California •

We Interrupt Your Regularly Scheduled Programming…,
White Columns, New York, New York;
District of Columbia Arts Center, Washington, D.C. •

**1991**
Comfort, Christopher Grimes Gallery,
Santa Monica, California

SITEseeing: Travel and Tourism in Contemporary Art,
Whitney Museum of American Art, Downtown
at Federal Reserve Plaza, New York, New York •

To Wit: Timely Objects with Ironic Tendencies,
Rosa Esman Gallery, New York, New York

**1990**
New Work-New York, Helander Gallery, Palm Beach, Florida

Satellite Intelligence: New Art from Boston and San Diego,
Museum of Contemporary Art, San Diego, California;
MIT List Visual Arts Center, Cambridge, Massachusetts •

Summer Group Show, Gracie Mansion Fine Art,
New York, New York

**1989**
PaintForum, Euphrat Gallery,
De Anza College, Cupertino, California

Drawings by Artists We Like, Dietrich Jenny Gallery,
San Diego, California

**1988**
Fate of the Animals, Worth-Ryder Gallery,
University of California, Berkeley

Summer Group Show, Dietrich Jenny Gallery,
San Diego, California

**1986**
UCSD/SDSU Exchange Show, Flor y Canto Gallery,
San Diego State University

Exhibition Series for Emerging Artists,
Galveston Arts Center, Galveston, Texas

Artists Guild Open Juried Exhibition,
San Diego Museum of Art, San Diego, California

**1985**
Seventh Annual Spring Arts Exhibition,
Austin Contemporary Visual Arts Association, Austin, Texas


**Public and Corporate Collections**

California Center for the Arts, Escondido, California

Delaware Museum, Delaware, Maryland

Museum of Contemporary Art, San Diego
La Jolla, California

Prudential Corporation, Newark, New Jersey

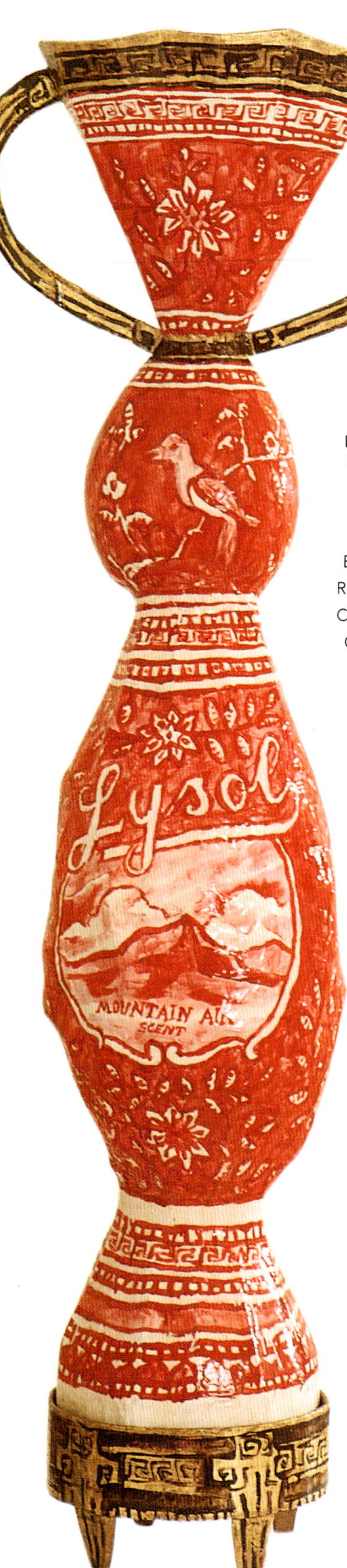

**Lysol Urn,** 1994

## Board of Trustees
## 2000–2001

Barbara Arledge

Dr. Mary Bear

Barbara Bloom

Ronald L. Busick

Christopher C. Calkins

Charles G. Cochrane, M.D.

August Colachis

David C. Copley

James S. DeSilva

Sue K. Edwards

Dr. Peter C. Farrell

Carolyn P. Farris

Pauline Foster

Murray A. Gribin

David Guss

Dr. Paul Jacobs

Beatrice Williams Kemp

Mary Keough Lyman

Robert J. Nugent

Maria E. Nuñez

Mason Phelps

Dr. Carol Randolph

Colette Carson Royston

Nora Desloge Sargent

Robert L. Shapiro

J. Anthony Sinclitico III

Matthew Strauss

Ron Taylor

Gough Thompson

Victor Vilaplana

## Staff

### Administration

Hugh M. Davies The David C. Copley Director
Charles E. Castle Deputy Director
Trulette Clayes CPA, Controller
Joyce Corpuz Executive Assistant
Kathlene J. Gusel Administrative Assistant
Sonia Manoukian Administrative/Special Projects Assistant
Robin Ross Accounting/Personnel Clerk

### Curatorial

Elizabeth N. Armstrong Senior Curator
Max Bensuaski Assistant Preparator
Allison Berkeley Curatorial Assistant
Tamara Bloomberg Research Assistant *
Allison Cummings Registrarial Assistant
Miki Garcia Lila Wallace Curatorial Intern
Gwendolyn Gómez Community Outreach Coordinator
Mary Johnson Registrar
Toby Kamps Curator
Doriot Negrette Lair Curatorial Coordinator
Kelly McKinley Education Curator
Ame Parsley Preparator
Gabrielle Wyrick-Bridgeford Education Programs Assistant

### Development

Anne Farrell Director of Development and Special Projects
Jane Rice 21st Century Campaign/Major Gifts Director
Laura Brugman Development Assistant
Kraig Cavanaugh Data Entry Clerk *
Michelle Gellner Development/Membership Assistant
Becky Judson Membership Coordinator
Synthia Malina Development Manager
Tamara Wiley Corporate Giving Officer

### Events, Visitor Services, Marketing/Public Relations

Jini Bernstein Events and Visitor Services Manager
Jon Burford Event Manager
Laurie Chambliss Public Relations/Marketing Assistant
Pamela Erskine-Loftus Museum Events Coordinator
Sandra Kraus Events and Visitor Services Assistant *
Jennifer Morrissey Public Relations Officer
Jana Purdy Marketing Manager *
Mike Scheer Production Manager
Event Managers *

### Retail Services

Jon Weatherman Manager of Retail Services
Michelle Thomas de Mercado Assistant Bookstore Manager
Delphine Fitzgerald Bookstore Clerk
Bookstore Clerks *

### Facilities and Security

Drei Kiel Museum Manager
Shawn Fitzgerald Museum Attendant
Tauno Hannula Facilities Assistant
David Lowry Chief of Security
Javier Martínez Site Manager, MCA Downtown
Ken Maloney Museum Attendant
James Patocka Facilities Assistant
Nicholas Ricciardi Receptionist/Telecommunications Coordinator
Demitrio Rubalcabo Museum Attendant/Receptionist, MCA Downtown
Jessica Windsor, Receptionist MCA Downtown *
Museum Attendants *

* part-time